Care, Cooperation and Activism in Canada's Northern Social Economy

Care, Cooperation and Activism in Canada's Northern Social Economy

Frances Abele
& Chris Southcott,
Editors

Polynya Press

An imprint of the University of Alberta Press

Published by

The University of Alberta Press
Ring House 2
Edmonton, Alberta, Canada T6G 2E1
www.uap.ualberta.ca

Library and Archives Canada Cataloguing in Publication
Library and Archives Canada Cataloguing in Publication

Care, cooperation and activism in Canada's northern social economy / Frances Abele & Chris Southcott, editors.

Includes bibliographical references and index.
Issued in print and electronic formats.
ISBN 978-1-77212-087-5 (paperback).
—ISBN 978-1-77212-110-0 (epub).
—ISBN 978-1-77212-111-7 (mobi).
—ISBN 978-1-77212-112-4 (pdf)

1. Cooperation—Canada, Northern—Case studies. 2.Cooperative societies—Canada, Northern—Case studies. 3. Native peoples—Canada, Northern—Social conditions—Case studies. 4. Native peoples—Canada, Northern—Economic conditions—Case studies. 5. Canada, Northern—Social conditions—Case studies. 6. Canada, Northern—Economic conditions—Case studies. I. Abele, Frances, author, editor II. Southcott, Chris, author, editor

HD3448.C39 2016 334.0971
C2016-904354-1 C2016-904355-X

First edition, first printing, 2016.
First printed and bound in Canada by Friesens, Altona, Manitoba.
Copyediting and proofreading by Kirsten Craven.
Indexing by Stephen Ullstrom.

The University of Alberta Press is committed to protecting our natural environment. As part of our efforts, this book is printed on Enviro Paper: it contains 100% post-consumer recycled fibres and is acid- and chlorine-free.

The University of Alberta Press gratefully acknowledges the support received for its publishing program from the Government of Canada, the Canada Council for the Arts, and the Government of Alberta through the Alberta Media Fund.

Government of Canada Gouvernement du Canada

Canada Council for the Arts Conseil des Arts du Canada

Alberta Government

Contents

Acknowledgements

We would like to acknowledge the contributions made to this volume by collaborators in the social economy organizations profiled here, for their patience with researchers' inquiries and their open-minded and open-hearted approach to working with the Social Economy Research Network of Northern Canada. Thank you to the authors in this volume for their interest in building a portrait of an oft-overlooked corner of northern social, economic and political life. Kelly Black of Carleton University, and Linda Cameron, Duncan Turner, Kirsten Craven and the staff of the University of Alberta Press helped us to make the book clear, while Valoree Walker held the enterprise together as she has done on so many of our projects, while expertly curating the photographs. Frances Abele thanks George Kinloch for inspiration, and for his unstinting intellectual and domestic support. Chris Southcott thanks Laura Hope-Southcott for her understanding and support throughout the project.

Base funding for the Social Economy Research Network for Northern Canada was provided by the Social Sciences and Humanities Research Council of Canada.

Frances Abele and Chris Southcott

Introduction

Few regions have experienced the degree of rapid economic change that northern Canada has over the past one hundred years. Communities that have long relied upon harvesting from the land and sea are now part of territorial economies dominated by the industrial exploitation of natural resources. They face an uncertain future in a globalized economy dominated by accelerating international trade and knowledge-based economic institutions. These changes, and accompanying state policies, have resulted in tremendous social and economic stress. With accelerating development pressures, northerners face both new challenges and opportunities to benefit.

New forms of self-government offer the potential for political empowerment, but they will not automatically deliver economic or social empowerment. Northern economies are dependent economies, increasingly shaped by large-scale mineral development. In this circumstance, Aboriginal organizations and governments and the territorial and federal states may play both a buffering and a facilitating role. Northern political innovations and new institutions are central to these roles: for example, demands for local participation in environmental and development decisions and the rise of resource co-management arrangements have opened space for consideration of economic alternatives, discussed and debated in a variety of fora.

In this book, we draw attention to some aspects of the northern political economy that have not, generally, been topics of discussion when people ponder the North's economic future—even though these often overlooked institutions are effective participants in northern political life, while others provide a wide range of services that are essential to northern societies' well-being. Collectively, these institutions are the northern social economy. The term "social economy" is used in a variety of senses in Canada; in the North, the term has two somewhat complementary meanings.[1] For our purposes in this volume, social economy is understood as an extension of what in the past has been termed "community economic development." It seeks to offer, and legitimate, a third aspect of economic development that in the past has been pushed aside in favour of large-scale, private-sector resource development and state-based initiatives. It refers to a strategy to develop and enhance the vitality, and the social and educational capital, of northern communities through organizations that are more directly controlled by the communities themselves. The social economy refers to those institutions in the community that are neither primarily profit-oriented nor state-driven. It refers to organizations whose primary purpose is to serve social goals in the community and whose structures are based on participatory democratic principles.

The chapters in this special collection are linked to the establishment of a network of researchers and northern community organizations looking into the potential of social economic development in Canada's North. Research done by this network is concentrating on the ability of social economic organizations to deal with several key political and economic characteristics that dominate the economies of northern communities. What our research has shown is that when they work together, individuals in northern communities can be extremely innovative and effective in providing solutions to many of the challenges the region is facing. While they often have few resources to mobilize, community groups have time and time again proven to be able to provide necessary services to meet their needs. This book presents a series of case studies that we believe illustrate the ways that community groups in Canada's North are using whatever limited resources are at hand to organize themselves to solve the economic and social problems they face. We hope this book will help convince others that given more resources, some of the best answers to what communities in the region need can come from the communities themselves.

The Social Economy: Questions of Identification

The term "social economy" is not widely used in northern Canada, and indeed in much of Canada outside Quebec. The term has been less frequently used than its close synonym, "community economic development" (Lévesque & Mendell, 2004; Chouinard & Fairbain, 2002). The central notion of both these terms is that they include economic activities that are not state-driven and not profit-driven. They include a large "third sector" that is often ignored (Quarter, 1992).

There is no firm consensus about the definition of the social economy, even among close colleagues in the same project (Southcott & Walker, 2009; Natcher, 2009; Abele, 2009). Most analysts would agree, though, that social economy organizations have in common the characteristic that obtaining a return on capital is not their primary purpose. They are, by nature, part of a stakeholder economy, whose enterprises are created by and for those with common needs and accountable to those they are meant to serve. They are generally managed in accordance with the principle of "one member, one vote." They are flexible and innovative and most are based on voluntary participation, membership and commitment. With respect to the North, we intend the definition to include traditional land-based activities, co-operatives, voluntary organizations, unions, and other activities whose primary purpose is not for profit or for the state

(Bouchard, Ferraton, & Michaud, 2006). This collection, though, focuses on social economy *organizations*, and not upon the social economy that characterizes many contemporary Aboriginal communities. Research on this expression of the social economy has been published elsewhere (see Southcott, 2015).

Thus, the social economy that is portrayed in this collection is made up of organizations in the not-for-profit sector that seek to enhance the social, economic and environmental conditions of communities. They use the tools and some of the methods of business, usually on a not-for-profit basis, to provide social, cultural, economic, health and other services to communities. Types of social economy organizations in Canada's North are retail and artistic co-operatives, political action and advocacy organizations, recreational and cultural organizations, nonprofit organizations, the voluntary sector, charities, foundations, credit unions and other social enterprises. They operate in areas ranging from housing to communications, and in areas such as recycling, home care, forestry, restaurants, catering, Aboriginal economic development and manufacturing. These enterprises are flexible and sustainable tools that allow communities to address objectives related to social and economic concerns while furthering goals of community participation and control.

The Social Economy and the Canadian North

The role and use of social economy organizations is unique in the North given the region's particular conditions. Historically, the North has been characterized by two types of communities: resource-dependent communities dominated by settler societies and Indigenous communities characterized by a mixed economy (Southcott, 2003). Other analysts (Bone, 2003) have noted that there is a third type of community—the service sector community. While none of these exist as a "pure" type, the three-way typology is useful for characterizing the ranges of economic bases in northern towns and cities. In each setting, the social economy takes a somewhat different form, and further, each type of community experiences large-scale natural resource exploitation in a different way (House, 1981; Bone, 2003; Chabot, 2004, Niezen, 1993; Stabler, 1990).

Three features of the northern economy create a significantly different context for social economy organizations. The first is the existence of a mixed economy in the region's predominantly Indigenous communities. Communities rely not only on wages from labour but on the continued existence of subsistence hunting, gathering and fishing activities, along with associated subsistence-based commodity production (traditionally tanned hides, furs, art and handicrafts). The next characteristic is the continued importance of the state in Canada's North. A colonial culture and the post-war implementation of paternalistic welfare state policies has meant a strong role of the state in the northern economy; the specifics of public finance and high northern costs mean that federal public expenditures will be important for many years to come. Finally, the dependence on large-scale resource exploitation found in northern resource-dependent communities will have deep and far-reaching consequences for all areas of northern community life, including the scope and foci of social economy organizations.

Researching the Potential of the Social Economy in Northern Canada

In 2006, a grant from the Social Sciences and Humanities Research Council of Canada (SSHRC) provided funding for a northern social sciences research network to study the potential for the development of the social economy in northern Canada. This grant was part of a larger SSHRC initiative to create a regionally diverse, Canada-wide initiative on the social economy.[2] SSHRC's initiative, in turn, responded to and complemented federal and territorial policy initiatives during the early years of the twenty-first century to develop an improved policy and program environment for "the third sector"—including what came to be called the social economy (Brock, 2001; Phillips & Levasseur, 2004). With the change of government in 2006, federal support for the third sector suddenly diminished and in the years following was steadily withdrawn. These events provided the backdrop for the research that is reflected in this volume.

The main objective of the Social Economy Research Network of Northern Canada, or SERNNoCa, was to create a network of university and college-based researchers and representatives of community-based organizations, operating as partners, to conduct research relevant to the social economy in Canada's North. In addition, the overarching objectives of the program were to support research, and help mobilize new knowledge, that will help develop social economy capacity in northern communities; contribute to defining policies by evaluating government policies and programs applicable to the social economy; improve the performance of organizations and enterprises in areas that are important to the social economy in Canada's North; demonstrate through, for example, inventories, statistics and comparative analyses the actual and potential contribution of the social economy to the various sectors of the economy of Canada's North; contribute to a northern perspective on debates relating to sustainable development; develop northern Canada's international contribution to, and visibility in, areas relevant to the social economy; and ensure the development of research capacity and the training of northern students in the area of the social economy through their participation in research projects and through the development of curricula.

From 2006 to 2012, the network conducted research in the three territories, Nunavik and Labrador organized around four research themes. The first theme was the conceptualizing, cataloguing and evaluating of the northern social economy. The other three themes are related to the specific characteristics underlying the social economy of the North as discussed above. SERNNoCa funded over thirty research projects involving fifty researchers and hundreds of community organizations. Research workshops, symposia and forums were held in all regions of Canada's North. The case studies highlighted in this book are only a sample of the many stories that were collected during the research conducted by SERNNoCa. They were selected based on their representativeness, not necessarily on their success compared to others. They are stories that we have collected that illustrate what can be done in the region when communities decide to act together.

Notes

1. See articles in the 2009 special edition of the *Northern Review* and especially Abele (2009), Natcher (2009) and Southcott and Walker (2009).
2. See http://socialeconomyhub.ca/.

References

Abele, F. (2009). The state and the northern social economy: Research prospects. *The Northern Review, 30*, 37–58.

Bone, R. (2003). *The geography of the Canadian North: Issues and challenges* (2nd ed.). Don Mills, ON: Oxford University Press.

Bouchard, M., Ferraton, C., & Michaud, V. (2006). *Database on social economy organizations: The qualification criteria* (Working Papers of the Canada Research Chair on the Social Economy Research Series—no R-2006-03). Montreal, QC: Université de Québec à Montréal.

Brock, K. (2001). Democracy is coming: The new interest in NGOs, civil society and the third sector. *The Philanthropist, 16*(4), 263–271.

Chabot, M. (2004). Consumption and standards of living of the Quebec Inuit: Cultural permanence and discontinuities. *The Canadian Review of Sociology and Anthropology, 41*(2), 147–170.

Chouinard, O., & Fairbain, B. (2002). L'économie sociale au Canada hors Québec: La tradition coopérative et le développement économique communautaire. *Économie et solidarités, Revue du CIRIEC-Cañada, 33*(1), 51–56.

House, J.D. (1981). Big oil and small communities in coastal Labrador: The local dynamics of dependency. *The Canadian Review of Sociology and Anthropology, 18*(4), 433–452.

Lévesque, B., & Mendell, M. (2004). The social economy: Diverse approaches and practices. Ottawa: Social Sciences and Humanities Research Council of Canada.

Natcher, D. (2009, Spring). Subsistence and the social economy of Canada's Aboriginal North. *Northern Review, 30*, 69–84.

Niezen, R. (1993). Power and dignity: The social consequences of hydro-electric development for the James Bay Cree. *The Canadian Review of Sociology and Anthropology, 30*(4), 510–529.

Phillips, S., & Levasseur, K. (2004). The snakes and ladders of accountability: Contradictions between contracting and collaboration for Canada's voluntary sector. *Canadian Public Administration, 47*(4), 451–474.

Quarter, J. (1992). *Canada's social economy*. Toronto, ON: Lorimer.
Southcott, C. (2003). Spacially based social differentiation in Canada's future: Trends in urban/non-urban differences in the next decade. In D. Juteau (Ed.), *Social differentiation patterns and processes* (pp. 205–252). Toronto, ON: University of Toronto Press.
Southcott, C. (Ed.). (2015). *Northern communities working together: The social economy of Canada's North*. Toronto, ON: University of Toronto Press.
Southcott, C., & Walker, V. (2009, Spring). A portrait of the social economy in northern Canada. *Northern Review, 30*, 13–36.
Stabler, J. (1990). A utility analysis of activity patterns of native males in the Northwest Territories. *Economic Development and Cultural Change, 39*(1), 47–60.

1

Matthew Beaudoin

Them Days

Them Days is an archive and magazine whose mandate is to keep "the history of Labrador alive by documenting and preserving the old ways and early days of Labrador" (Them Days Inc., 2009). Based in Happy Valley-Goose Bay, Them Days strives to serve the interests of Inuit, Innu, Labrador Métis and Settler inhabitants throughout Labrador. Its offices house the archive and publication facilities for the magazine. Them Days also has a website (www.themdays.com), which allows people to search the archive's holdings, and a separate blog (themdays.wordpress.com) maintained by the staff to highlight the daily activities at the archives.

Them Days is an unconventional social economy institution in that it is not devoted to housing, social enterprise, community economic development or small-scale manufacturing (Quarter, Mook, & Richmond, 2003; Southcott, 2009). Archives and magazines are rarely discussed in the social economy literature, yet Them Days' efforts to record, preserve and disseminate the heritage of Labrador warrant attention from students of the social economy. As noted by Diamantopoulos (2014), alternative forms of public media can be effective means to challenge hegemonic mass media outlets and benefit the social aspects of society. Them Days is locally produced, operating with public, private, business and volunteer support; its activities work to directly increase the social capital in the broader Labrador community. It contributes to increasing awareness of local heritage, creating a shared knowledge base and advancing community pride. Considering the Aboriginal and political context of Labrador, the preservation and dissemination of the local heritage has the potential to make a major contribution to Labrador society. As such, even though Them Days does not fall within the traditional "third sector" institutions that are often considered part of the social economy, it is a not-for-profit organization that responds to the urgent needs of the local community and can thus be understood within a social economy context (Laville, Lévesque, & Mendell, 2006; Lévesque, 2003; Mook, Quarter, & Ryan, 2010).

History

Them Days magazine was proposed by Isaac Rich, a retired trapper, in 1973 as a Labrador Heritage Society project to present stories and photographs collected by Rich in Labrador communities. Rich observed that Labrador lifeways were changing and the stories told by Labrador Elders were an important connection between the shifting present and a deeper Labrador heritage. The Elders' stories that Rich and others grew up with recorded a way of living that had already passed; Rich and his collaborators saw that as these Elders aged and passed on, the stories could be lost.

The original plan was to produce a single issue of the magazine. In 1975, the Old Timers League, a seniors' organization, received funds from the federal New Horizons for Seniors Program to produce the publication. The first edition of the magazine was published in August 1975. Due to community interest and an increasing number of collected stories, *Them Days* rapidly became a quarterly magazine. *Them Days* continued to operate under the umbrella of the Labrador Heritage Society until it was incorporated

1.1 Photographs from a photo-identification event with Elders, 2010.
Courtesy of Aimee Chaulk

on November 10, 1980. Since then it has operated as a nonprofit organization run by a volunteer board of directors.

The Them Days Labrador Archives were established in 1984. The archives became a repository for numerous audio and video recordings, historic papers and photographs. The collections consist of records created by the contributors of the magazine and donations by individuals, businesses and organizations that understood the heritage value of their holdings. These collections, along with the present-day efforts to continue to collect stories and knowledge of the contributors, form the backbone of *Them Days* magazine.

Founding editor Doris Saunders spent nearly thirty years in the position. During her term, *Them Days* grew from a single, sixty-four-page issue into the quarterly publication that continues today. Saunders was originally hired in 1975 as the editor for the inaugural issue, but her role rapidly broadened to include conducting interviews, research, writing and production of the magazine. Saunders was also heavily involved in fundraising for *Them Days* and often went without pay to ensure that funding was available to produce the magazine (Markham, 2006). The extreme efforts that Saunders contributed to *Them Days*, and Labrador society as a whole, were formally recognized in 1986 when she was inducted into the Order of Canada and in 1994 when she received a honourary doctorate of letters from Memorial University of Newfoundland. Since Saunders's 2003 departure from the position of editor, there have been several editors of the magazine, the most recent being Tara McLean and Aimee Chaulk.

Impact on Community

Labrador Inuit and Labrador Innu stories have played a role in Them Days, but the early period saw a particularly heavy focus on the Labrador Métis and Settler stories of southern Labrador. The Settlers are people considered to be of European descent who occupied the southern Labrador coast. However, European men living in Labrador had been intermarrying with local Aboriginal (almost entirely Inuit) women for generations (Kennedy, 1997). Many Settlers thus chose to identify themselves as the Labrador Métis, forming the Labrador Métis Association in 1985. In this context, Settlers are self-described and recognized to be a people of mixed heritage intimately connected with the Labrador landscape.

This group filed a land claim in 1991, changed its name to the Labrador Métis Nation in 1998 and, later, to NunatuKavut. *Them Days*' focus on Labrador Métis stories emerged from Saunders's own personal interest and connections to the people within these communities. Within general histories, the Labrador Métis or Settlers were often omitted or ignored and their stories, traditions and lifeways overlooked (Kennedy, 1995, p. 90). As such, *Them Days* emerged as a local source of publicly disseminated knowledge that confronted this gap in the popular discourse. Numerous ethnographies of Labrador society were published before the existence of *Them Days* (e.g., Ben-Dor, 1966; Zimmerly, 1975), but at that time only two were written by Labrador authors (McLean, 2006). In many ways, *Them Days* helped change many longstanding attitudes about the Labrador Métis and Settler peoples and set the stage for their political organization.

If the early publications placed a particular emphasis on the stories of the Labrador Métis peoples, more recently *Them Days* has sought to record the stories of Labrador society as a whole and fill in many of the knowledge gaps. The most apparent omission was the stories of the Innu (First Nations) of Labrador (Fitzhugh, 1999, p. 377), and efforts have been made to record and include more materials related to the Innu.

Them Days magazine and archives has proven to be an invaluable resource for members of the Labrador and academic community. Community members refer to the archives as a genealogical database, a record of land use for land claims negotiation and a source of information relating to past lifeways. The holdings of recorded interviews and photographs comprise one of the most extensive collections of this sort in Labrador. The holdings simultaneously act as a reference collection for community members and researchers and as a repository for original and copied materials. The importance of the repository role was underlined recently after a fire in the northern community of Nain destroyed the Nunatsiavut (Labrador Inuit government) archive. Them Days' extensive and broad archive was able to return copies of many lost materials to help re-establish the destroyed collection. Them Days archive and magazine has also become an important resource for authors and scholars. Them Days plays a significant role for many publications related to Labrador society and history (Fitzhugh, 1999; Kennedy, 1995; Rompkey, 2003), and it is not uncommon for articles from *Them Days* magazine to figure prominently in graduate student work related to Labrador. *Them Days* magazine has become an accessible resource for scholars who research a wide array of topics related to Labrador.

More recently, Them Days has undertaken the stabilization and digitization of its present holdings, including *Them Days* magazine. This ensures the continued existence of the material for subsequent

1.2 Jenna Bridges (Katimavik volunteer) and Aimee Chaulk (Editor) at an Expo Labrador booth, promoting Them Days to businesses interested in working in Labrador, June 2010.
Courtesy of Aimee Chaulk

generations and eases the sharing of information with others. Volunteers at the archive are undertaking these projects, with assistance through joint ventures and fundraising opportunities with partners like Memorial University and McGill University.

Reasons for Success

There are many reasons for Them Days' success. The most important factor is probably that this grass roots organization was conceived, designed and implemented by the Labrador community for the

Labrador community. Individuals such as Rich and Saunders were vital to the early work of Them Days, but their efforts would have been in vain without community support. Them Days' existence has relied on volunteers in the creation of articles, as both contributors and interviewees, and for the physical production of the magazine. The magazine is filled with contributions from volunteers who write about their own families and experiences. It is because Them Days continues to resonate with the Labrador community that it is able to support itself with volunteers and contributors.

Them Days emerged during a time when many people in Labrador were divided, both politically and culturally, and many voices felt silenced. During the 1970s, there was an increase in political activism in Labrador. The Labrador Innu and the Labrador Inuit established their own organizations, the Naskapi Montagnais Innu Association in Labrador and the Labrador Inuit Association, respectively, to advocate for their rights. In a sense, Labrador was divided between Labrador Inuit, Innu and Settler/Métis who were all striving to demonstrate their cultural heritage, so that history had a new salience for all.

The Them Days archive is a significant contribution to Labrador society because of its role in continuously collecting and housing stories and records for future generations. However, the success of the archive is tied to the success of *Them Days* magazine. *Them Days* became a method to disseminate and share the stories, histories and pictures that were housed at the archives within the Labrador community. The pieces in *Them Days* were generally short, thematically varied and contained black and white photographs. Effectively, the magazine distilled knowledge and history held in community memories into easily accessible and engaging pieces. These pieces were written specifically to be accessible, enjoyable to read and easy to share. This format allowed for *Them Days* to gain acceptance and popularity in many Labrador homes. The archive became the caretaker of the collection, but the magazine was the means by which the knowledge within the collection was returned to the community.

1.3 Them Days new office building constructed in 2009 in Happy Valley-Goose Bay, NL.
Courtesy of Aimee Chaulk

Future Obstacles

The greatest future obstacle for Them Days is related to funding. The securing of continued and reliable funding remains a perennial problem for Canadian social economy organizations (Karaphillis, Moore, & Asimakos, 2010). Them Days continues to operate as a nonprofit organization that derives its operating budget from government grants, fundraising events, donations, royalties and subscriptions. These funding sources have been extremely helpful in covering the cost of constructing and maintaining the building that houses the archives, the quarterly printing of the magazine and specific archival projects, such as the ongoing digitization project, but money for the hiring and retention of staff is more difficult to obtain. Presently, much of the work at Them Days is undertaken by volunteers, as there are only two paid positions. The staff and volunteers are engaged, energetic people who believe strongly in the value of Them Days, but the resources to hire and train more staff, as well as more professionals, are currently unavailable. As with many non-profit community organizations, salaries are low and come with few benefits. This makes it difficult to retain employees and impossible to attract the experienced professionals that such an organization requires. For example, the archive has a great facility and equipment but lacks an archivist to support current staff in developing the archive to its full potential. Them Days has been successful in securing funding for its current level of operations, but it is unlikely that this will change for the foreseeable future.

Conclusion

The future of Them Days relies on the ability of staff and volunteers to continue to be successful in securing funding and recruiting volunteers. The drive and need for the organization is as strong as ever and there are continuously new stories to record. The efforts of Them Days to record the stories of the past are ongoing, but as lifeways continue to change, a new set of storytellers and stories are emerging and need to be recorded.

Them Days emerged in a very specific historical context that contributed to its persistence and success. It has balanced the collection and preservation of materials in the archive with the dissemination of knowledge in the magazine. Local community members understood that contemporary histories were missing the importance of the knowledge maintained by Elders in the communities. Through their efforts and community support, they were able to record and preserve an important part of the living heritage of Labrador. This persistence and community support demonstrates that Them Days has a very important role to play within the social economy of Labrador (Chaulk, 2011). Them Days' relationship within Labrador society is unique and would be difficult to find in many other contexts. Them Days expands our understanding of how social economy organizations can benefit the societies in which they are embedded.

Author's Note

I would like to thank Robin McGrath for meeting with me and discussing the history and activities of Them Days Inc., as well as Scott Neilsen for hosting me during my stay in Happy Valley-Goose Bay. I would also like to thank Chris Southcott and Frances Abele for their insightful edits and suggestions for this chapter.

References

Ben-Dor, S. (1966). *Makkovik: Eskimos and settlers in a Labrador community.* St. John's, NL: Memorial University.

Chaulk, A. (2011, March). Them Days Inc. *Labrador symposium on the social economy.* Symposium conducted at Happy Valley-Goose Bay, NL. Retrieved from http://yukonresearch.yukoncollege.yk.ca/sern/events/labrador

Diamantopoulos, M. (2014). On breaking a wild young colt: Associative intelligence, alternative journalism and the cultural mutualisation of the Canadian Prairies. *Journal of Co-operative Studies, 47*, 39–55.

Fitzhugh, L.D. (1999). *The Labradorians: Voices from the land of Cain*. St. John's, NL: Breakwater.

Karaphillis, G., Moore, S., & Asimakos, S. (2010). *Financing social economy organizations.* Victoria, BC: Canadian Social Economy Research Partnerships.

Kennedy, J.C. (1995). *People of the bays and headlands: Anthropological history and the fate of communities in the unknown Labrador.* Toronto, ON: University of Toronto Press.

Kennedy, J.C. (1997). Labrador Métis ethnogenesis. *Ethnos*, *62*, 5–23.

Laville J-L, Lévesque, B., & Mendell, M. (2006). *The social economy: Diverse approaches and practices in Europe and Canada*. Montreal, QC: Alliance de recherche universités-communautés en économie sociale, Université du Québec à Montréal.

Lévesque, B. (2003). Mondialisation, démocratie plurielle, économie sociale et solidaire [Special issue]. *Économie et Solidarités*, 103–121.

Markham, N. (2006). Remembering Doris. *Them Days, 30*, 15–19.

McLean, W. (2006). "Dr. Dot," an appreciation. *Them Days, 30*, 24–31.

Mook, L., Quarter, J., & Ryan, S. (2010). What's in a name? In L. Mook, J. Quarter, & S. Ryan (Eds.), *Researching the social economy* (pp. 3–24). Toronto: University of Toronto Press.

Quarter, J., Mook, L., & Richmond, B.J. (2003). *What is the social economy?* (Research Bulletin #3). Toronto, ON: Centre for Urban and Community Studies, University of Toronto.

Rompkey, B. (2003). *The story of Labrador*. Montreal, QC: McGill-Queen's University Press.

Southcott, C. (2009). Introduction: The social economy and economic development in northern Canada. *The Northern Review, 30*, 3–11.

Them Days Inc. (2009). *Them Days: Stories of early Labrador*. Retrieved from http://www.themdays.com/

Zimmerly, D.W. (1975). *Cain's land revisited: Culture change in central Labrador, 1775–1972*. St. John's, NL: Memorial University.

2

Matthew Beaudoin

Labrador Friendship Centre

During the 1960s and 1970s, the Province of Newfoundland and Labrador's centralization program compelled large numbers of Aboriginal residents of Labrador to relocate from coastal and remote communities to more urban centres (Kennedy, 1995, pp. 188–190). Happy Valley-Goose Bay was a pre-existing regional hub that had developed around Canadian Forces Base Goose Bay. Inhabited mainly by people of Euro-Canadian heritage, Happy Valley-Goose Bay became one of the major receiving communities for this influx of relocated people. Many Innu were relocated to the nearby settlement of Sheshatshiu, while Labrador Inuit and Métis[1] were relocated to Happy Valley-Goose Bay itself. Happy Valley-Goose Bay is a wage-based population centre, and the history and activities of the Labrador Friendship Centre are typical of social economy organizations in such locations; it is a not-for-profit organization that is engaged with both a market and non-based social economy to respond to the urgent needs of the local community (Laville, Lévesque, & Marguerite, 2006; Lévesque, 2003; Mook, Quarter, & Ryan, 2010). The Labrador Friendship Centre emerged to answer the social needs of the Happy Valley-Goose Bay community

2.1 The Robert C. Lyall Labrador Friendship Centre in Happy Valley-Goose Bay, NL, 2011.
Courtesy of Valoree Walker

created by the large influx of a largely rural population into an urban context during the centralization program.

The Labrador Friendship Centre's mandate is to "endeavour to provide the best possible services to enrich the lives of the Inuit, Innu and Métis of Labrador through the provision and implementation of social, cultural, health, education, employment, and developmental initiatives" (Labrador Friendship Centre, 2009). The centre is associated with the National Association of Friendship Centres (NAFC), providing programs and services targeted toward, but not exclusive to, Aboriginal peoples living in and near the community of Happy Valley-Goose Bay. The Labrador Friendship Centre's main facility houses offices, a hostel, a cafeteria, a local craft shop (Drumdancer Arts & Crafts Shop) and the community food bank. It is an example of a local, not-for-profit organization that works with various levels of government, private businesses and community needs—an effective lens through which to observe the social economy in Happy Valley-Goose Bay.

History

In 1973, activists from the Company of Young Canadians and the Happy Valley Inuit Association began discussions to address the difficulties many relocated peoples were having in adjusting to the new landscape. They saw the need and undertook the steps to establish a Friendship Centre in Happy Valley-Goose Bay that would act "like a bridge which tries to bring together two different ways of life" (Happy Valley Inuit Association, 1973). These steps included obtaining community interest and approval, support from various levels of government and preparing an application to the National Association of Friendship Centres. The NAFC movement itself had emerged during the increased urbanization of the mid-1950s, which highlighted the need for specialized services for Aboriginal people who were living in cities (NAFC, 2010). The NAFC was established in 1972 with the mission of being the primary provider for programs and services targeting urban Aboriginal peoples. Over time, the NAFC movement grew and developed; in 2005, it identified its role as "an efficient means to fight against poverty and social exclusion since it generates economic and social wealth" (Coalition of Native Friendship Centres of Quebec, 2010). Presently, the NAFC connects over one hundred communities, supports a wide variety of social programming and facilitates numerous academic research projects (Graham, 1998; Lavallee and Poole, 2010; Thurston, Oelke, & Turner, 2013).

Many of the early activities engaged the Labrador Inuit in Happy Valley-Goose Bay, but from the outset the Labrador Friendship Centre was conceived to support all of the Aboriginal people who were moving to the community. The organization they envisioned would help newcomers to Happy Valley-Goose Bay adapt to life in the new community by providing counselling and referral services, social and recreational programs, cultural awareness and community development to address problems of verbal communication, "lack of housing, employment, transportation problems, and problems with alcohol and the law" (Labrador Friendship Centre, 2009). These efforts were to help the new residents to adjust to life within their new community, as well as to try to improve the community overall. The organization received its initial funding in 1974 and held its first general assembly in 1975, where it elected its founding president, Robert Lyall. The Labrador Friendship Centre has continued to operate with this same mandate and intent.

Impact on Community

The Labrador Friendship Centre has had an important impact on the urgent and immediate needs of the Happy Valley-Goose Bay community, while simultaneously offering services and training programs oriented toward the future. The centre offers programs for adult basic education, infant/child health, housing, job searches and placements and adult continuing education (e.g., computer courses). The hostel provides an affordable and safe (i.e., secure, alcohol- and drug-free) place for temporary residents of Happy Valley-Goose Bay to stay. In housing the local food bank, the centre provides a reliable and accessible source of food for people in need. The programs at the centre target specific needs identified by the community or governmental bodies. It is difficult to quantify the specific impacts these services have on the community, but they are continuously used by community members. As the largest not-for-profit organization in Labrador, the Labrador Friendship Centre is also a significant employer within the community and has often been cited as an example of organizational best practices (Oliver, 2011).

Reasons for Success

The reasons for the success of the Labrador Friendship Centre are based in its ability to provide targeted programs and support for individuals in the community. This is a result of administrative

2.2 The Robert C. Lyall Labrador Friendship Centre in Happy Valley-Goose Bay, NL, 2011. Lyall was a founding member and the first president of the centre.
Courtesy of Valoree Walker

design, success in obtaining funding and programs and the realistic assessment of the needs within the community. These three factors are encompassed within the centre's funding structure.

The centre's success in maintaining funding can be attributed to its situation and perspective. The role of the administrative staff is to run the day-to-day operations of the organizations, conduct fund-raising and continuously apply for new sources of funding. A large portion of funding is received from the NAFC as an annual lump sum grant that is provided to all the friendship centres in Canada that fall within the NAFC's mandate. This grant is a significant and welcome source of money for the Labrador Friendship Centre. However, the value of the grant has not changed in many years and has not been adjusted to meet the growing and changing needs of the centre. A second source of the centre's funding comes from a variety of sources that include charitable fundraising, revenues from room rentals, hostel and cafeteria services and earnings from the Drumdancer Arts & Crafts shop. It must be noted that the revenues from these sources are minimal and cover the cost of operating these services rather than amassing funding for other programs. The third and, arguably, most significant source of funding for the centre is provided through the hosting of programs and services funded by governmental or private organizations. The Friendship Centre has the capacity to assist these programs through its local knowledge of the community. These programs are developed to address specific community issues (e.g., HIV/AIDS, youth services, adult education, housing services, etc.) and have associated staff positions, administrative budgets and operational funding that are used to deliver the programs. Many of the programs housed by the Labrador Friendship Centre are developed by an external body, but because of its success and reputation, the centre is able to effectively cooperate with the Innu Nation, the Nunatsiavut government and the NunatuKavut association.

There are, however, some difficulties associated with the administrative architecture and funding structure. Since programs and funding are provided by an external body, Friendship Centre staff must continuously reapply to host these programs, expending a significant amount of administrative effort. Also, inefficiencies arise because there is no guarantee of long-term funding. As the objectives and financial perspectives of the external body shift, so do the programs. This has the potential to create an inherent instability and generate a difficulty in long-term planning. A similar pattern of instability and program shifting has been previously noted within the National Association of Friendship Centres structure (Edgar, Marshall, & Bassett, 2006, p. 13). To date, programs have generally been offered over several years, but the risk of drastic and unforeseeable program shifts remains. Moreover, funding is pre-allocated for specific purposes. This pre-allocation is designed to promote the specific targets of the program but often does not account for the realities of program implementation within the community, creating further difficulties in effectively providing the program. This pre-allocation often requires the Labrador Friendship Centre to use its own resources to fill the financial gaps within the program. To mitigate this, staff members work to deliver programs that can operate in tandem and support each other.

Future Obstacles

The Labrador Friendship Centre staff indicates they have continuously maintained a forward-looking perspective and that they have understood the necessity to adjust their programs and foci to meet the needs of their community. The staff continues to show a willingness to attract and host a variety of programs that address the ever-changing community dynamic and needs. For example, an HIV/AIDS project was sponsored by the Labrador Friendship Centre in response to a lack of information available to many Aboriginal communities in Labrador. The centre must continuously develop innovative ways to attract funding for existing programs. They can often use complementary funding streams (e.g., governmental, private, business and private fundraising) to better support the implementation of programs that would be beyond the means of any single funding source. Presently, the centre is able to meet many of the community's needs, but staff are aware of the necessity of expansion. With the almost inevitable implementation of major resource development projects, most notably the Lower Churchill Hydroelectric Project, people and money will flow into the region and with this influx there will be associated negative social impacts (see Hodgkins, 2009). The Labrador Friendship Centre sees the need to continue to expand to address these future needs.

There exist two major obstacles for the future of the Labrador Friendship Centre. The centre's building has reached capacity and there is a lack of administrative funding. Presently, the centre is operating at the functional capacity for its facilities. It has expanded its current building (the Robert C. Lyall Building), run programs out of its former building, rented space from neighbouring buildings and used space at local organizations such as the College of the

North Atlantic. More program opportunities are available to provide support for the community, but the Labrador Friendship Centre has run out of viable options to house further programs. To effectively support further programming, the centre will need to acquire more space or new buildings, a task that is becoming more difficult due to the rising cost of land and housing in the area. Renting space is an option, but the increased costs and difficulties of finding spaces suited to the specific needs of the administration and operation of programming remain difficult. Future donations of space or funding for the acquisition of space will be required within the near future.

The other major obstacle to the continued expansion of the Labrador Friendship Centre is the lack of core funding to cover administrative costs. Current financial resources are able to pay the salaries of the staff that administer programming. Specific program coordinators are often allocated with a successful bid for a program, but the administration staff provided by the centre handles the integration of the programs within the existing structure, the co-ordination between programs and the day-to-day operations of the organization. These staff members have the added responsibility of seeking new programs, fundraising and supporting the relationship between the organization and the community.

Conclusion

The Labrador Friendship Centre is a vital part of the Happy Valley-Goose Bay community and directly affects the lives of many individuals within the community. It has established its organization in a manner that sustains itself by providing programs that fit within its mandate. These programs are delivered in an efficient and effective approach that directly assists the community. The centre has earned a positive local reputation and the support of government funders. Without this support, both societal and financial, the centre would not be able to operate as it has and would be a much less effective means of helping the community.

There is always uncertainty with any organization that relies on government funding; program criteria could shift or funding could become scarce. The centre is well aware of these uncertainties and has organized itself to operate, and thrive, in a fluid situation. Continued growth and expansion of programs is a testament to its ability to understand and use the system in which it is embedded. While it is encountering an expansion plateau, the centre continues to develop novel and future-oriented methods to obtain new sources of funding and support that will allow for the continued delivery and expansion of the programs within its mandate. It is likely that the Labrador Friendship Centre will continue to expand and maintain its place as a fixture within the Happy Valley-Goose Bay community.

Author's Note

I would like to thank Jennifer Hefler-Elson for meeting with me and discussing the history and activities of the Labrador Friendship Centre, as well as Scott Neilsen for hosting me during my stay in Happy Valley-Goose Bay. I would also like to thank Chris Southcott and Frances Abele for their helpful edits and suggestions for this chapter.

Note

1. At the time of relocation, the term "Settler" was used to refer to people of mixed European-Inuit heritage; however, post-1985 the term "Labrador Métis" was adopted instead. Because Labrador Métis is the preferred term today, it will be used throughout this paper instead of Settler.

References

Coalition of Native Friendship Centres of Quebec. (2010). *Aboriginal social economy circle*. Retrieved from http://www.rcaaq.info/en/social-economy/aboriginal-social-economy-circle.html

Edgar, L., Marshall, C., and Bassett, M. (2006). *Partnerships: Putting good governance principles in practice.* Ottawa, ON: Institute on Governance.

Graham, K.A. (1998). Urban Aboriginal governance in Canada: Paradigms and prospects. *Zeitschrift für Kanada-Studien, 18*, 77–89.

Happy Valley Inuit Association. (1973, December). *Voice of the Inuit Newsletter*. Happy Valley-Goose Bay, NL: Author.

Hodgkins, A.P. (2009, Spring). Re-appraising Canada's northern "internal colonies." *The Northern Review, 30*, 179–205.

Kennedy, J.C. (1995). *People of the bays and headlands: Anthropological history and the fate of communities in the unknown Labrador*. Toronto, ON: University of Toronto Press.

Labrador Friendship Centre. (2009). *Labrador Friendship Centre: Enriching Aboriginal life in Labrador.* Retrieved from http://www.lfchvgb.ca/home/

Lavallee, L.F., & Poole, J.M. (2010). Beyond recovery: Colonization and healing for Indigenous peoples in Canada. *International Journal of Mental Health and Addiction, 8*, 271–281.

Laville, J-L, Lévesque, B., & Mendell, M. (2006). *The social economy: Diverse approaches and practices in Europe and Canada*. Montreal, QC: Alliance de recherche universités-communautés en économie sociale, Université du Québec à Montréal.

Lévesque, B. (2003). Mondialisation, démocratie plurielle, économie sociale et solidaire [Special issue]. *Économie et Solidarités*, 103–121.

Mook, L., Quarter, J., & Ryan, S. (2010). What's in a name? In L. Mook, J. Quarter, & S. Ryan (Eds.), *Researching the Social Economy* (pp. 3–24). Toronto, ON: University of Toronto Press.

National Association of Friendship Centres (NAFC). (2010). *Our history: The friendship centre movement*. Retrieved from http://nafc.ca/history.htm

Oliver, S. (2011, March). Labrador Friendship Centre. *Labrador symposium on the social economy*. Symposium conducted at Happy Valley-Goose Bay, NL. Retrieved from http://yukonresearch.yukoncollege.yk.ca/sern/events/labrador

Thurston, W.E., Oelke, N.D., & Turner, D. (2013). Methodological challenges in studying urban Aboriginal homelessness. *International Journal of Multiple Research Approaches, 7*, 250–259.

3

Jean-Sébastien Boutet

Torngat Fish Producers Co-operative

A Social Fishery Venturing off the Coast of Northern Labrador

The Torngat Fish Producers Co-operative Society is a fish purchasing and transforming operation that was established in December 1980 by northern Labrador fishers from the predominantly Aboriginal communities of Nain, Davis Inlet, Hopedale, Makkovik, Postville and Rigolet. Today, the co-operative processes snow crab, Greenland halibut (turbot) and Arctic char at its two fish plants in Makkovik and Nain.

Torngat's incorporation under the Newfoundland Co-operative Societies Act was a response to the 1978 decision by the provincial government led by Conservative Premier Frank Moores (1972–1979) to offload its responsibility of the region's fish plants to the private sector.[1] At the time, the Moores administration looked for outside companies to place tenders on leasing and operating the commercial fishery's infrastructure. Alarmed by the prospect of a private appropriation of the plants—whose management, it was feared, would be governed by the logic of financial profitability rather than that of long-term community welfare—and nurturing a sense that the commercial fisheries belonged to the people of the north coast, local residents, supported by the Labrador Inuit Association (LIA), formed the Fisheries Emergency Policy Committee with the goal of reversing the impending takeover. The main outcome of this emergency response was a rough proposal to create a co-operative fishing organization in northern Labrador.

An overwhelming majority of coastal residents provided backing for this unusual and somewhat ambitious idea through popular referenda that were held in each of the six communities before Newfoundland and Labrador's Department of Rural, Agricultural and Northern Development signed off on the official certificate of registration. As Torngat's first elected president, Alex Saunders, explains, if the technical concept of a "co-operative organization" was perhaps novel for the Aboriginal peoples of the region, certainly the practice of sharing resources and responsibilities communally was not a new idea. Despite lacking entrepreneurial experience at the time, the original Torngat founders proved resilient and resourceful in their ability to get the co-operative rapidly off the ground—and the fishery out of private hands. This moment at the turn of the 1980s is unique in the history of resource exploitation in northern Labrador. Notwithstanding the fact that the company has faced continuous challenges through more than three decades of operations (some of which were grave enough that they threatened its very survival), the co-operative project enabled local people to regain a certain level of sovereignty over a fishery that had long evaded their control, having been exploited primarily by and for interests exogenous to the Labrador coast.

The formation of Torngat by the Emergency Committee was encouraged by federal Minister of Fisheries and Oceans Roméo Leblanc. In 1979, Minister Leblanc allocated a new deep sea shrimp licence covering Davis Strait and the north coast of Labrador, in effect granting offshore rights to the Labrador Inuit Association after specifying that the allotted quota was to be harvested by a company organized under a *co-operative* management structure. Upon its inception (which quickly followed and in fact sought to take advantage of the initial shrimp licence allocation), Torngat did not own any fishing vessels, which meant that the company had to rely on freezer trawlers such as Denmark-based *M.V. Ocean Prawns* to harvest its shrimp quota—a reliance on foreign charters that has mostly persisted to the present day (Figure 3.1). By the summer of 1980, nearly half a year before the official incorporation of the Torngat co-operative, the Danish shrimp trawler had begun harvesting the quota held in trust by the LIA, and up to six Inuit labourers were employed aboard the vessel. The royalties earned with the support of foreign boats from the original licence contributed significantly, along with some federal help such as Canada Manpower's Local Employment Assistance Program secured during the early stages, to the co-operative's ability to establish its business. Most notably, it enabled Torngat to reallocate shrimp-derived surpluses into new experimental and more risky ventures that proved vital for the organization's growth and survival through the years. In this sense, Leblanc's decision to allot the shrimp quota was crucial for Torngat's historical development and for the expansion of its membership; still today, the co-operative remains dependent on the health of this offshore fishery to maintain its important inshore operations.

Through its first decade of operations, Torngat ran its main freezing and processing plant in Makkovik, in addition to managing a small char landing station in Davis Inlet, feeder plants in Hopedale and Postville (the latter included a salting fish operation) and a buying and handling facility in Rigolet. As with many other fishing ventures, the co-operative was severely affected by the moratoria and fishing restrictions on cod and salmon put in place by Canada in 1992. The federal government introduced these desperate policies in order to address the near collapse of commercial stocks across the northwestern Atlantic fisheries of the Grand Banks and the Newfoundland and Labrador continental shelf (Dempson et al., 2001;

3.1 Danish commercial vessel harvesting the shrimp quota for Torngat, ca. early 1980s.
Courtesy of Torngat Fish Producers Co-operative Society

Rose, 2007). Less than two decades after the establishment of the two-hundred-mile exclusive economic zone, initially implemented in 1977 "as a protectionist measure for the national fisheries" of Canada and the United States (among other states with territorial waters), and as recognition of these countries' "right to manage all fisheries within a 200-mile zone," it became clear that the move toward state ownership of fish had failed to deliver on conservation grounds (Kurlansky, 1998, p. 181; Rose, 2007, p. 427). More broadly, many have pointed to poor scientific planning as the main cause for the collapse of the fisheries, perhaps even going so far, according to more radical voices, as implicating technique and the ecological bureaucracy for managing the Atlantic fisheries into "annihilation" (Bavington, 2010). In this regard, fisheries observers and critics have noted that the decrease of groundfish populations was a well-known fact of life to inshore fishers, but also according to several biologists, which long preceded the official 1992 moratoria (Finlayson & McCay, 1998). Yet in the period leading up to the collapse, overfishing by outside fleets continued, producing few tangible returns for the local Aboriginal communities whose sea-based wealth steadily flowed out of their own waters.

Unfortunately, the complex Department of Fisheries and Oceans population models could not quite incorporate empirical observations and perceptions from the grassroots, and warning calls about unhealthy stocks went more or less unheard until the closure (Finlayson & McCay, 1998). Among many repercussions, the federal government's decision to shut down the fisheries soon led to the abandonment of Torngat's once-thriving Rigolet venture. The plant ceased its operations in 1998, with corresponding loss of crucial employment for the community (Figure 3.2); this was a salmon-handling facility that, early on, the co-operative argued had "created more jobs in the fishery than was ever created in Rigolet before" (where, for instance, up to eleven people were employed by Torngat in 1981) (Torngat, personal communication, February 2012). As another consequence, the moratorium and fishing restrictions forced Torngat to diversify its production and to experiment with innovative markets—some more fruitfully than others—by exploiting alternate species and establishing niche productions. In 1995, the Nain plant came under the management of Torngat, and since that year the co-operative has obtained its most consistent returns from the shellfish business, particularly following the introduction of successful scallop and snow crab productions at the newly acquired Nain factory (Figure 3.3) and in Makkovik, respectively (Figure 3.4). If the crab venture has generally operated profitably ever since, scallop production recently encountered some difficulties, and as a result the Nain plant has not marketed any scallop products on a commercial scale since 2007 (Figure 3.5). In addition to shellfish, Torngat continues to process Arctic char and Greenland halibut, even though the economic viability of these two fisheries is particularly fragile and poses recurrent challenges to the managers and members of the co-operative.

3.2 Landed Weight of Salmon, Cod and Char at Rigolet Plant, 1982–1998

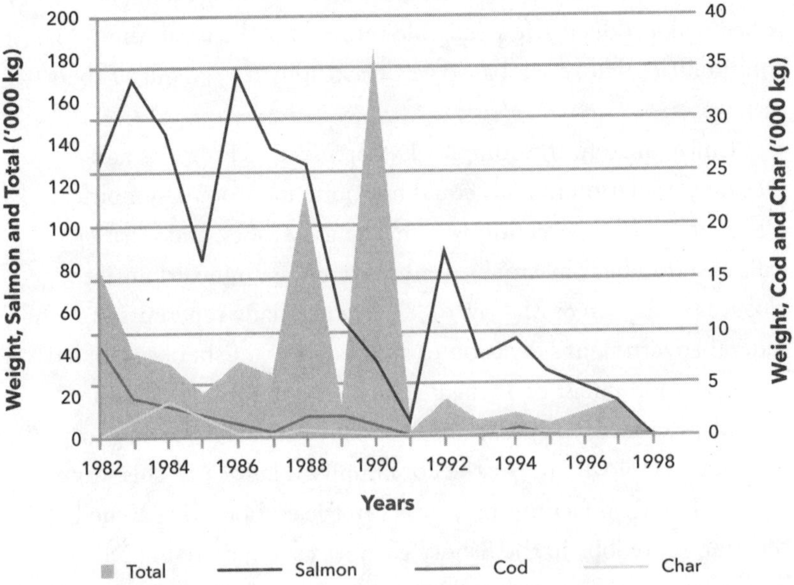

3.3 Nain fish plant during the off-season, January 2015.
Courtesy of Jean-Sébastien Boutet

3.4 Makkovik fish plant, June 2012.
Courtesy of Christina Goldhar

3.5 Landed Weight of Scallops, Char (Nain), Snow Crab and Turbot (Makkovik) 1995–2011

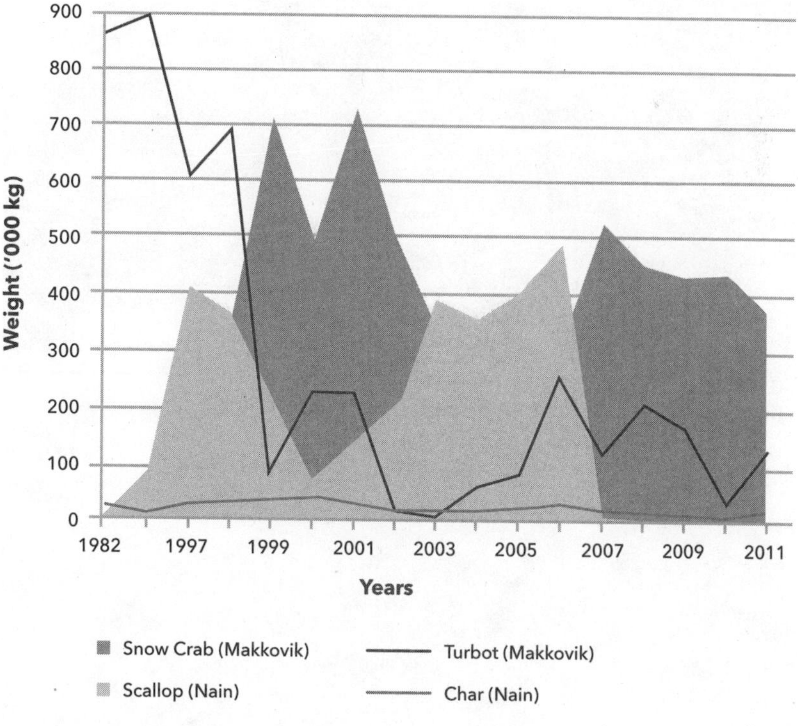

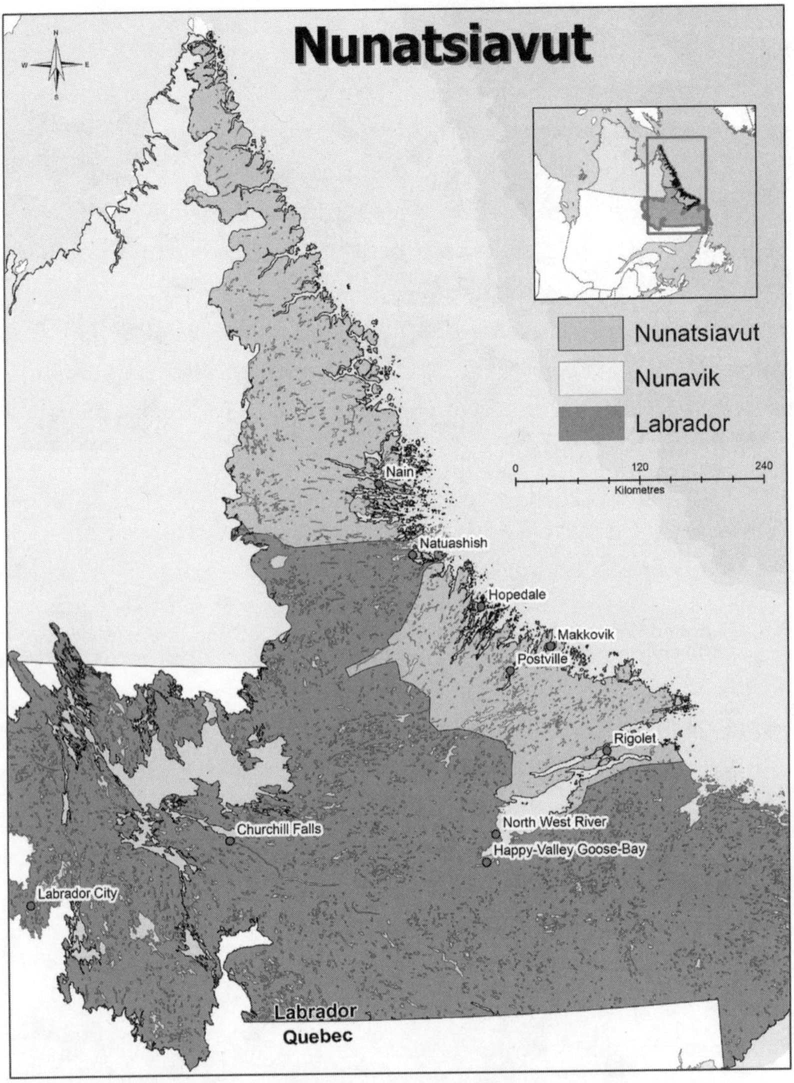

3.6 Territory covered by the Labrador Inuit Land Claims Agreement.
Courtesy of the Nunatsiavut government

Over the past three decades, the co-operative has grown to include over 650 members, most of whom are residents of the provincial Torngat Mountains electoral district who are involved in one way or another with the fishery, either as plant workers, fishers, collector boat workers or relatives thereof. A large proportion of these members are Inuit beneficiaries of the Labrador Inuit Land Claims Agreement, an accord that was signed in 2005 between the LIA and federal and provincial authorities to recognize the Inuit right to self-governance on their northern Labrador homeland of Nunatsiavut (Figure 3.6). If some 80 to 90 per cent of its members identify as Nunatsiavummiut, or Nunatsiavut Inuit, the fishing society can also involve nonresidents of the Torngat Mountains district (including nonbeneficiaries of the land claims agreement) who are licensed to fish in northern Labrador, as well as groups such as government bodies and nonprofit organizations that have their head office in Labrador or even registered co-operatives operating worldwide. Membership in the co-operative is obtained through a monetary subscription in the form of capital shares; though this is not mandatory, in practise these shares are mostly held by individuals.

Since its creation in the early 1980s, the purpose of the co-operative has been to work for the economic development of Labrador's coastal communities by means of fulfilling the aims and objectives inscribed in its constitutional bylaws. In particular, Torngat seeks to promote on a co-operative basis the interests of the electorate from the Torngat Mountains district; to act on behalf of the society members as the selling agents for their fishing products; to operate buildings, machinery, plants and vehicles, as well as to acquire and use leases, concessions and fishing rights, and to rent, purchase, sell and trade goods and equipment necessary to promote the economic welfare of its shareholders; to effect insurance against risk, loss or accident to its members; more generally, to promote the co-operative movement through joint ventures and undertakings, cooperation and association with other registered co-operative societies; and, finally, to conduct educational work among its members in order to attain the aforementioned goals (Torngat Fish Producers Co-operative

Society Limited, 2006). Nowadays, the co-operative mainly serves the five Inuit communities of Nunatsiavut. Although Davis Inlet (now Natuashish) still has a handful of members registered with the co-operative, they have been mostly inactive in the commercial fishery since Canada imposed the salmon fishing restrictions in 1992. As a result, this Innu community where Torngat used to purchase salmon before shipping it to Nain for processing is no longer officially considered part of the co-operative's domain of operation.

The Torngat co-operative is typically not in a position to pay out financial dividends to its members at the end of the fiscal year. Therefore, the main benefits it offers to the people of Torngat Mountains are crucial opportunities for seasonal wage employment and the presence of a purchasing outlet for local fishers (other marginal advantages include a reduction on the purchasing price of finished products, which can be bought directly from the fish plants or from the Happy Valley-Goose Bay head office [Figure 3.7], as well as modest economic spinoffs for communities that welcome fishing boats throughout the summer months). Regarding employment, members are normally given priority over nonmembers. On average, the co-operative has hired over four hundred individuals seasonally (about 220 plant workers and 180 fishers), with the best season registered almost two decades ago when 414 people laboured at the Makkovik and Nain plants, while 549 fishers sold their catch to Torngat during the summer of 1998. The second half of the 1990s indeed represented the heyday of the company in terms of the absolute number of people employed (332 plant workers and 301 fishers on average between 1996 and 2000), and that number has been diminishing since, in part due to tightening market conditions and the firm restrictions on quotas. As a result, the most recent five-year period of 2006–2010 has seen a 44 per cent decrease in the number of workers employed with respect to the most successful half decade of operations (1996–2000). In parallel, the number of fishers selling their products to the co-operative has followed a similar downward trend throughout the recent years (a 57 per cent decrease from 2006 to 2010 compared to 1996–2000), with correspondingly lower benefits accruing to Nunatsiavut communities (Figure 3.8).

3.7 Torngat Fish Producers Co-operative Society headquarters in Happy Valley-Goose Bay, February 2012.
Courtesy of Jean-Sébastien Boutet

3.8 Total Number of Plant Workers and Fishers Employed by Torngat, 1981–2011

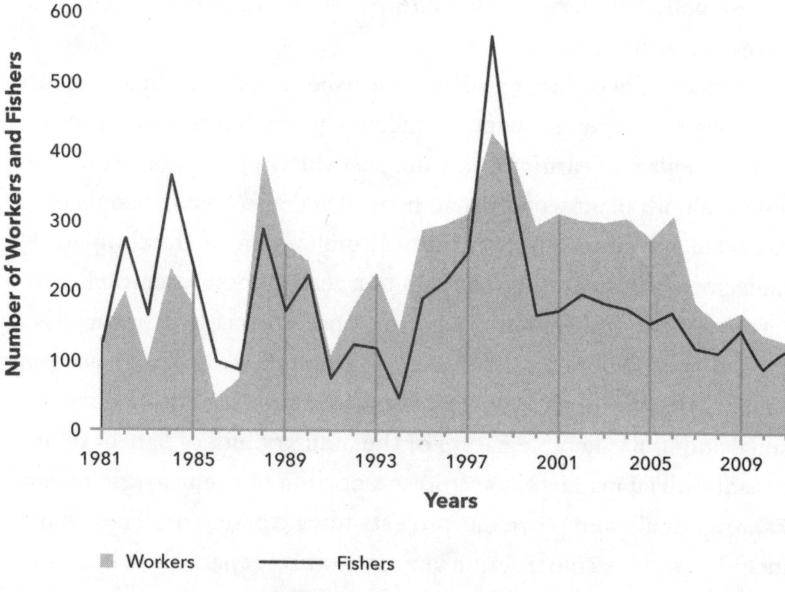

From a strict economic point of view, operating a commercial fishery co-operative on the Labrador north coast presents numerous challenges but also some opportunities. For Torngat, the difficulty to stay financially afloat and continue to support people's fishing livelihoods in the region has certainly been compounded by the communitarian and caring nature of the enterprise, although, paradoxically, it can also be estimated that these very qualities of the organization have contributed perhaps most significantly to its impressive longevity. If, on the one hand, the society's management and operational structure do not directly prevent Torngat from competing on an equal footing with private enterprises on international fishing markets, on the other hand its social mission as outlined in the constitutional bylaws has had a marked influence on local harvesting and processing choices. Rather than relying on a pure "bottom line" mentality motivated by financial profits, Torngat's officials also seek to consider the potential effects of their business decisions on Nunatsiavut communities. As such, the (more straightforward and seemingly "rational") option of eliminating least profitable ventures from the overall company operations is rarely considered the most desirable, even though, in the end, Torngat is occasionally left with no other alternative but to move away from a particular fishery.

Since the activities of all Torngat fisheries provide much needed employment in Nunatsiavut (cumulatively worth nearly seventy-five million dollars in earnings over the past thirty years, when considering both plant workers and fishers) and also enable people to maintain and actualize important cultural practices, the co-operative managers can usually consent—up to a certain loss-generating level—to absorb deficits through the more profitable departments such as the offshore shrimp fishery. In brighter years, they have even sought, as a way of giving back or compensating for the highly seasonal and unpredictable nature of the industry, and as part of their broader social mandate, to redirect a portion of their margin toward creating smaller employment projects for the members. These have included various construction ventures, wharf repairs, building of a community boardwalk, retailing and resupplying of goods to fishers along the coast and fish stocks monitoring contracts. As Torngat President Tony Wolfrey illustrates, "We used to be a real social company, helping people. These days we can't really do that, because of financial reasons" (personal communication, February 2012). Yet because of the remarkable challenges associated with operating a commercial fishery in the region, General Manager Keith Watts maintains that very few fisheries strictly bound by standard accounting could ever make it for as long as Torngat has. In this particular sense, the company's co-operative constitution and its sensitivity to community well-being have proved to be a veritable lifeline for the north coast fishery, especially through the most turbulent (post-moratoria) years.

The wild char fishery in Nain is one concrete example of a venture that Torngat operates with a social conscience first. Unlike other fisheries, Torngat holds sufficient quotas to make it a viable enterprise. But consumer markets are underdeveloped for this species, making it difficult to sell the transformed products, and on the supply side it is always a test for Torngat to compete with the cheaper farmed char—sold for up to a dollar a kilogram cheaper—that originates from different regions of Canada or the rest of the world. In spite of a sharp decrease in the output of the Arctic char fishery in the past five years, Watts still argues that this operation must be sustained because "it's something that is very close to the heart of Inuit on the north coast, it's their way of life. So we are the ones who are keeping the char fishery alive, even at its current low production level. We're not giving up on it" (personal communication, February 2012). In this regard, an interesting historical anecdote relates back to a period in the early 1980s when the company, still in its infancy, encouraged Inuit fishers to move north because of a reduction in Arctic char stocks around Nain, a region that had been overfished due to the presence of an active fish plant there. While the project of running a Faroese freezer boat in Saglek Bay for a season was hardly beneficial from a strict financial standpoint (more than two thousand dollars a day were spent on charter expenses,

3.9 Private fishing camp established at the west end of Hebron, ca. 1990–1991. During this period, the Newfoundland and Labrador government ran a collector service that would bring fish harvested from this area down to Nain for processing.
Courtesy of Billy Duffett

for instance), it allowed a handful of Inuit fishers to return to their former settlement and fishing grounds near Hebron (Figure 3.9). At least in social terms, Torngat considered it a very successful experiment, even remarking at the time on the area's high potential and expressing the need to further concentrate fishing efforts there in future seasons. For Alex Saunders, with these northern undertakings the co-operative "wanted to do something for the people that were forcibly resettled from Hebron....The venture north, although very meaningful and spiritual for the Inuit, was not a sound business proposition, [but] in the end it all proved worthwhile" (personal communication, February 2012).

In more recent years, by contrast, the company went through further streamlining and decided to abandon its small Arctic char business in Hopedale—no char has been landed there since 1997—and return the infrastructure to the provincial authorities in order to better focus their resources on the Nain operations, where production levels also had to be reduced in the past decade in order to minimize deficits (since char is typically sold at a loss). Above all, the profitability of the Torngat co-operative is vulnerable to the relatively short fishing season that is a function of harsh weather conditions. In the Nain area, for instance, at most six weeks of fishing are usually available, so that in any given season Torngat is typically one of the last crab fisheries to come on stream in Canadian waters because of the unfavourable sea ice conditions. As a result, the marketplace is already well occupied when the co-operative is in a position to finally sell its finished products. Other constraining factors are the prohibitive costs associated with running commercial fishing activities in remote environments, notably in the domain of energy, shipping and storage. Since the fish products cannot be trucked out of the region, they need to be cold-stored until they are shipped to Lewisporte, on the island of Newfoundland, where they are destined for international markets that are mainly located in the eastern United States and Asia. In a context where net prices are thus never optimal, unpredictable transportation delays due to weather—a frequent occurrence in northern Labrador—often lead to a further drop in selling prices that can prove decisive. Of course, these challenges are compounded by the normal vagaries of international fish markets. Since almost a decade ago, when the value of the Icelandic scallop industry bottomed out, Torngat has ceased to market this species because the price offered became lower than what fishers were generally willing to harvest for. This inopportune situation developed in spite of the venture's resounding success in preceding years and notwithstanding the fact that much like char, quota level and stock numbers are not restricting factors for scallop availability and thus for the overall viability of this fishery in the Nain area. Similarly, Torngat's rock cod production, which reached twenty-seven thousand kilograms in 2007 (and as high as 119,000 kilograms in the early 1990s), was negatively affected by a sudden collapse of the salt cod market, and the co-operative was since forced to abandon this operation based in Postville.

The difficulty of securing good and reliable quotas is a constant challenge for Torngat in at least a few of its fisheries. Although operating a profitable snow crab operation out of Makkovik, the co-operative, along with the Nunatsiavut government, holds a relatively small 450-ton designated quota for the species (attributed historically by the Department of Fisheries and Oceans to the LIA as a result of intensive activism; this quota has since been reduced to 310 tons), which means that in most summers crab is harvested out after only a few weeks of fishing. Regarding the Greenland halibut fishery, the situation is even more dire, since Torngat has been unable—despite years of lobbying the federal government and with knowledge of good summer access to turbot stocks off the north coast—to obtain an inshore communal (designated) quota, which could greatly improve the co-operative's productivity. If Torngat is usually able to buy a considerable amount of turbot from southern fishers who are harvesting competitive quotas, these purchases remain quite unpredictable; the extreme price-sensitive nature of the industry makes it difficult for Torngat managers to forecast how much fish nonmember harvesters will be landing in Nunatsiavut in a given summer. The lack of designated quotas has therefore meant that even though the co-operative is equipped with facilities to process large quantities of fish—it landed several hundred tons annually through most of the 1990s—the output of the turbot fishery has been oscillating erratically for at least the last decade.

The attribution of additional communal quotas is vital for the long-term sustainability of the fishery, according to the current co-operative managers. Besides facilitating staff retention and providing a more solid foundation for the company to expand into new productions, this move would limit the daily uncertainties and allow Torngat to plan its activities more efficiently with regard to the harvesting periods, the quantity of fish to be purchased and processed and, therefore, the number of fishers who are willing or able to sell their catch to the co-operative. In this sense, quota restrictions and resulting production fluctuations have had a direct influence on the number of fishers and plant labourers that Torngat is in a position to employ every season. As the co-operative grows more dependent on nonmember fishers to harvest the competitive quotas, local employment conditions in the plants also risk further degradation.

From the fishers' point of view, the combined unreliability of fish markets and the insufficient quotas have led them to gradually abandon their boats, being no longer able to operate them profitably. Less than a handful of fishers working in the region today possess their own registered commercial vessel, another important factor that contributes to the instability of the fishery, according to Assistant General Manager Ron Johnson. The lack of steady fisher crews makes it difficult for the co-operative to diversify and adjust its production, which is a fundamental condition for running a vibrant fishery. As Johnson explains, even when you operate a profitable snow crab operation, there is always a need to develop new niche markets, if nothing else than as a precautionary measure to face future downward cycles (ecological or economic) that are characteristic of the fishing industry. This has been attempted recently on the south coast of Labrador, where scallop harvesters identified potential for establishing a sea cucumber fishery. "But if you don't have the staff already in place," Johnson remarks, "there is nobody there to get into these experimental ventures for new markets" (personal communication, February 2012). Maintaining the plant at full capacity and retaining a stable crew of workers and fishers who are offered competitive salaries and compensation has become a particularly pressing issue for Torngat managers, especially as some seasoned employees are leaving the commercial fisheries in order to seek more advantageous working conditions in other resource-based industries in Nunatsiavut or elsewhere in Labrador and northern Canada. This type of labour shortage is a complex phenomenon that evidently cannot be reduced to the lack of communal quota availability or industry cycles. During the 2014 season, for instance, Inuit fishers harvested turbot quotas, but the products could not be transformed at the main processing facility in Makkovik due the company's inability to attract plant workers there. Unattractive wages, insufficient accommodations needed to house nonresident workers and an inferred lack of interest in the processing industry by the younger generation were among the causes advanced to explain these recent shortcomings. Above and beyond these factors, Ron Johnson still concludes: "You have to have quotas to have a boat, and you have to have fishers to have a fish plant. You have to have enough species to fish and enough fishers to make the plant viable, to have the [fish plant] workers you need" (personal communication, February 2012).

For Torngat's former president, Alex Saunders, "northern Labrador has always been on the fringes of the commercial fishery" (personal communication, February 2012). Within this arduous geographic—but also economic and political—context, the prospects for the co-operative are difficult to assess. The future is hopeful but remains fragile, with the threat of closure always a possibility. Yet, fundamentally, current President Tony Wolfrey believes that "a lot of people don't want Torngat to be dissolved. They own it, you know. They feel proud to be a part of this company" (personal communication, February 2012). The Torngat co-operative has had a long history of working in the region to sustain the economic and cultural well-being of the people and the communities. As such, the co-operative has been willing to operate a social fishery that provides important employment for Nunatsiavut as long as the financial strain could at least be offset by more profitable species such as shrimp and now snow crab. In fact, the recent surge of this latter operation and the interesting prospects for ventures such as various crab species (including northern stone crab), whelk, seals and sea cucumbers, have contributed to fuel a wind of cautious optimism among the membership. In more recent years, Torngat management has moved to establish closer links with Nunatsiavut government officials (some cooperation already exists, in the form of a loan guarantee granted annually by the Inuit government to the co-operative in order to support commercial borrowing, for example) to coordinate lobbying efforts toward federal authorities who ultimately control much of the fate of the northern fishery. There is great hope that the formalization of this partnership will enable a better administration of quotas, guarantee a more solid representation for north coast fishers and plant workers and, as General Manager Keith Watts puts it, present "a cloak of respectability" (personal communication, February 2012). Yet, as many people may agree, fishing off the north coast of Labrador is inherently harsh and unpredictable, and this in some sense reiterates the need for a fishery organized and managed along social principles in this unusual environment. "I've been around almost since Torngat has been around, as a member," Wolfrey finally reflects. "And I know what it's like in the fishery, sometimes you have some really bad years, but some other times you'll have some really good years too. This year I hope is going to be that year" (personal communication, February 2012).

Author's Note

All statistical data are courtesy of Torngat Fish Producers Co-operative Society. I would like to thank Keith Watts, Ron Johnson, Tony Wolfrey and Alex Saunders for agreeing to share their knowledge and stories about Torngat, as well as Billy Duffett and Christina Goldhar for their photographic contributions. I am also grateful to Ron Sparkes of the Labrador Institute for his support in the early stages of this project. I am responsible for all remaining errors or omissions.

Note

1. The construction of this infrastructure was originally financed in part by the federal Department of Indian and Northern Affairs but also involved some funding from Aboriginal organizations.

References

Bavington, D. (2010). *Managed annihilation: An unnatural history of the Newfoundland cod collapse*. Vancouver, BC: University of British Columbia Press.

Dempson, J.B., Schwarz, C.J., Reddin, D.G., O'Connell, M.F., Mullins, C.C., & Bourgeois, C.E. (2001). Estimation of marine exploitation rates on Atlantic salmon (*Salmo salar* L.) stocks in Newfoundland, Canada. *ICES Journal of Marine Science, 58*, 331–341.

Finlayson, A.C., & McCay, B.J. (1998). Crossing the threshold of ecosystem resilience: The commercial extinction of northern cod. In F. Berkes and C. Folke (Eds.), *Linking social and ecological systems: Management practices and social mechanisms for building resilience* (pp. 311–337). Cambridge, UK: Cambridge University Press.

Kurlansky, M. (1998). *Cod: A biography of the fish that changed the world.* Toronto, ON: Vintage Canada.

Rose, G.A. (2007). *Cod: The ecological history of the North Atlantic fisheries.* St John's, NL: Breakwater Books.

Torngat Fish Producers Co-operative Society Limited. (2006, May 25). By-laws. Makkovik, NL.

4

Cédric Drouin and
Frédéric Moisan

Nunavik Creations

A long time before being used to perform religious ceremonies, to indicate social status or to demonstrate creativity in a fashion show, clothes were made to protect people from the weather. In circumpolar regions, the cold was a serious threat to survival. Inuit have developed very efficient clothes to protect themselves from the extreme cold of the Arctic. Dubuc (2002) describes one innovation that was used to protect against the cold, involving the construction of two garments superimposed, one with fur fit to the body and the other facing outward, to create a protective layer of warm air between them. Others historically sought Inuit knowledge regarding cold-weather clothing. For example, Inuit traded different garments with the Innu, including knee-length boots and parkas (Dana, 2010).

Nowadays, for Nunavik Creations (NC), an Inuit company based in Nunavik (northern Quebec), clothes production is at the heart of its business activities and reflects this historic legacy.

History

Nunavik Creations is a subsidiary company founded by Makivik Corporation (MC) in 2002. Makivik plays a fundamental role in Nunavik socio-economic development by acting as a promoter of various economic activities. It is a nonprofit organization created in 1975 to administer funds received from both the Canadian and Quebec governments after the signature of the land claim agreement, the James Bay and Northern Quebec Agreement (JBNQA).[1] Currently, MC has a broader mandate with its commitment toward the Inuit of Nunavik to protect their rights, interests and culture, and to stimulate economic development and employment, as well as to improve housing conditions (Makivik Corporation, 2011).

On its business side, MC has developed and funded a corporate system of commercial operations within eleven different subsidiary companies. Four are joint ventures and seven are wholly owned by MC. They are mandated to provide a business model aimed to enhance Inuit economic, social, cultural and professional interests. Nunavik Creations stimulates the regional economy by creating job opportunities, providing employment in the sewing workshops and stores, offering sewing work to seamstresses working at home and buying local products from the Inuit of Nunavik. Nunavik Creations also promotes the talent and the culture of the Inuit of Nunavik by selling standardized products reflecting these, and corresponding to the market needs in terms of quality, sewing standards and labelling. The Montreal head office of Nunavik Creations handles marketing, production, sales and distribution. It also houses a sewing centre; three others are located in Inukjuak, Kangirsuk and Salluit. These small factories provide equipment and materials to the sewers. The most popular retail items include sealskin vests and mitts (*pualuk*), slippers (*pinirak*), tuques (*nassak*), other hat styles in sealskin, parkas (*atirik*), parkas with a place in the back to carry a baby (*amautik*) and snow pants. There are also a variety of bags, including purses, packsacks, computer sleeves and briefcases, as well as books, agendas, Bible covers, portfolios and wallets.

The history of the company is shown briefly in the chronology of major events in Table 4.1 (L. Falardeau, general manager, Nunavik Creations, personal communication, December 2011).

4.1 Chronology of Major Events in Nunavik Creations' Company History

Year	Event	Nunavik Creations Activity
2002	Unveiling Inukshuk at Quebec National Assembly, Quebec City, QC	fashion show
2005	Festival of Desert Cultures & Civilizations, Dubai, United Arab Emirates	fashion show
2005	United Nations Framework Convention on Climate Change Conference, (Arctic Day), Montreal, QC	fashion show and production of uniforms for catering wait staff
2006	Coastal Zone Canada 2006 Conference and Youth Forum, Tuktoyaktuk, NT	fashion show
2006	McCord Museum, Montreal, QC	craft show
2007	Quebec International Pee Wee Hockey Tournament, Quebec City, QC	designed and produced the official parkas for the Nunavik team
2007 2009 2011	Puvirnituq Snow Festival, Puvirnituq, QC	fashion show and sales
2008 2010 2012	Northern Lights, Ottawa, ON, and Montreal, QC	trade show for sales, daily fashion shows and a gala fashion show
2010	Olympic Games 2010, Vancouver, BC	trade show
2011	Inuit Tapiriit Kanatami, Ottawa, ON	fashion show
2011	Truth and Reconciliation Commission (northern national event regarding the placement of Inuit in residential schools), Inuvik, NT	fashion show and sales

After ten years of existence, NC has enhanced its productions and refined its products by providing its employees with continuous training and purchasing computerized industrial equipment and sewing software. High-quality products and a fur clothing line are sold in luxury goods markets. NC has become a well-known leader among the sewers and independent artists of Nunavik, giving them visibility and promoting their talents through its participation in fashion and craft shows. Having achieved this developmental basis, NC is now entering a maturation phase with the possibility to compete on national and international markets.

Impacts on the Community

This section aims to illustrate Nunavik Creations' outcomes in terms of social economy through three main aspects—economy, culture and society—that have been improved, modified or ameliorated by its business activities.

NC has generated very interesting economic effects. Of prime importance, between 2007 and 2010, NC expended 85 per cent of its income (from sales and grants) on salaries and the purchase of local business services (such as transportation, promotion and training, among others). Salaries and other payments to individuals are a very important aspect of the business.

NC encourages women to visit the sewing centres and to learn how the products are made. Women have been invited to the sewing centres in Inukjuak and additional visits to Salluit, Kangirsuk and Kangiqsualujjuaq are planned (Makivik Corporation, 2009). Thanks to this program, Inuit in the communities will have better employability and more skills to work within the sewing industry. There is a training program to control the quality of the production. NC's workshop manager in Montreal, Vera Greening, said, "Most of our Inuit seamstresses come to us with some level of sewing skills acquired by using regular domestic sewing machines. Our first objective is always to transfer these skills to using regular industrial sewing machines and techniques for production of

4.1 Nunavik Creations sewing workshop in Ville St-Laurent.
Courtesy of Louise Faladeau

garments for the commercial industry" (personal communication, December 2011).

Another way of seeing the economic impact of NC is that the company purchases goods and services from the local and territorial economy. The points of sale in Kuujjuaq, and now in Inukjuak, act as distributors for the local seamstresses throughout Nunavik by buying and retailing their products to the residents (Inuit and non-Inuit) and to the travelling workers and tourists passing through by plane or boat. By paying freight and airfares, NC contributes to the revenue of the Inuit-owned airline that gives discounts or sponsors the various social activities in Nunavik. Overall, the presence of NC allows more pecuniary movement through Nunavik and brings more money to local households.

As it was briefly described in the introduction, sewing was and still is at the centre of the Inuit way of life. It's a part of

4.2 Working on one of the Nunavik Creations at the Inukjuaq workshop.
Courtesy of Louise Faladeau

Qaujimajatuqangit—Inuit traditional knowledge—as a historic productive activity. We have identified three aspects of NC's activities related to Inuit culture. Firstly, there is the inextricable link between hunting and sewing within Inuit communities. These two subsistence activities are deeply interdependent and MC aims to maintain this union. MC possesses a subsidiary specialized in taxidermy and tanning, Nunavik Furs. This taxidermy centre could be a supplier to NC in the future. The taxidermy centre is not a supplier yet because of a lack of workers causing a shortage in production. The taxidermy centre allows for the possibility of buying the skins and furs to be tanned from the hunters; NC would buy the tanned products from Nunavik Furs instead of buying them through southern auctions in order to produce the mitts, parkas and accessories.

Secondly, clothes production is related to the traditional female role. Driscoll-Engelstad (1997) noted "the interdependence of hunter and seamstress was such that a woman's prestige and economic value within a household rested largely on her sewing skills" (p. 26).

In this regard, NC helps to maintain a classic responsibility carried by women, as well as encouraging them to get more involved in the economic future of their community.

Finally, NC preserves and builds upon the traditional knowledge of the seamstresses as a traditional form of art. NC provides the place, equipment and tools to let seamstresses express themselves through the production of contemporary clothing. That gives Inuit women the chance to use clothes as a contemporary cultural representation (Driscoll-Engelstad, 1997).

Reasons for Success

The success of NC is based on three elements. First, there has been support from MC and from the Kativik regional government in the form of capital funding and training. Secondly, NC benefitted from the sewing knowledge and the number of seamstresses already present in Nunavik. This helped to get the first inventories in order to start retailing and brought various types of products and ideas. Now seamstresses work with a designer who guides their artistic sewing skills toward standardized garments and products. Thirdly, NC's active promotion of its products has built a reputation based on the authenticity of Inuit-made products made in Quebec with traditional materials.

Obstacles

Fugmann (2009) has identified four main challenges—location, workforce, infrastructure and markets—faced by corporations and private businesses in Canadian Inuit communities. We discovered that two of them—workforce and markets—were applicable in our case. We will discuss each of them, in order of importance.

First, NC faces two major problems regarding its workforce. The first major problem is that it has difficulty retaining seamstresses ("Nunavik Creations Review," 2007). In fact, the company is always looking for new employees in all of its production centres. Factors that create this shortage include the important role that Inuit women play at home and competition from other employers in their communities. The other problem involves training: while many are able to sew traditional clothes, fewer are able to design and produce new designs on the new equipment. The shortage of sewers has caused some uncertainties of supply, and there is a constant need for training on the new equipment.

The second major difficulty is related to market development. For NC, sufficient revenue cannot be generated by relying upon local buyers alone. According to Fugmann (2009), Inuit product company sales are affected by a limited local market due to the small population and the relative lack of discretionary income due to the high costs of living and frequent unemployment. While NC has corporate contracts for parkas, winter pants, mitts and promotional items, these are insufficient to sustain stable production throughout the year. NC is actively seeking other markets and has developed a web presence for global marketing.

Conclusion

The experience of Nunavik Creations has provided a viable model of a northern social enterprise. It seems clear that NC contributes positively to the communities' social economy, especially by increasing the income of some inhabitants and by stimulating land-based economic activities, particularly in terms of traditional clothes and handcrafted accessories production. Moreover, as General Manager Louise Falardeau explains: "Retailing the handcrafted clothes and accessories is one part of the operation. The main impact is to have an ongoing training to professionalize the seamstresses and the product and to offer these clothes and accessories on various markets. We want to strengthen the design of new contemporary products without neglecting the traditional products" (personal communication, December 2011). Overall, it appears to us that NC's socio-economic impacts are very valuable for women. Therein, they are getting more involved in community development, and it is also strongly positive for their own personal development.

Note

1. The JBNQA is based on two equally important founding principles. First, Quebec needs to use the resources of its territory, all its territory, for the benefit of all its people. Second, the government of Quebec must recognize the needs of the Native peoples, the Cree and the Inuit, who have a different culture and a different way of life from those of other peoples of the province (MDDELCC, 2002).

References

Dana, L.P. (2010). Nunavik, Arctic Quebec: Where cooperatives supplement entrepreneurship. *Global Business and Economic Review, 12*(1/2), 42–71.

Driscoll-Engelstad, B. (1997). Beyond anonymity: The emergence of textile artists in the Canadian Arctic. *Museum Anthropology, 20*(3), 26–38.

Dubuc, É. (2002, Fall). Culturelle matérielle et représentations symboliques par grands froids: Les vêtements de l'industrie du plein air et la tradition inuit. *Material History Review, 56*, 32–42.

Fugmann, G. (2009). Development corporations in the Canadian North—Examples for economic grassroots among the Inuit. *Erdkunde, 63*(1), 69–79.

Janda, R. (2005). Why does form matter? The hybrid governance structure of Makivik Corporation. *Vermont Law Review, 30*(3), 785–814.

Makivik Corporation. (2009). *Annual report 2008–2009*. Saint-Laurent, QC: Author.

Makivik Corporation. (2011). *Makivik corporation*. Retrieved from http://www.makivik.org

Makivik Magazine. (2004, Summer). Nunavik Creations review. *Makivik Magazine*, (69), 32.

Makivik Magazine. (2005, Winter). Nunavik Creations review: Arctic Day displays. *Makivik Magazine*, (75), 14.

Makivik Magazine. (2007, Summer). Nunavik Creations review. *Makivik Magazine*, (81), 27. Retrieved from http://collections.banq.qc.ca/ark:/52327/2165608

Makivik Magazine. (2011–2012, Fall–Winter). Nunavik Creations review: Who are you wearing? *Makivik Magazine*, (95), 48.

Ministère du développement durable, de l'environnement et de la Lutte aux changements climatiques (MDDELCC). (2002). Environmental assessment of northern projects. Retrieved from http://www.mddelcc.gouv.qc.ca/evaluations/mil-nordique/index-en.htm

5

Lucille Villaseñor-Caron

Unaaq Men's Association of Inukjuak

Inukjuak's Unaaq Men's Association is an example of how traditional economy skills are being put to use in a modern economy in ways that contribute to local and regional social and economic development and well-being. Since 2001, the association has paired local Elders with youth to teach traditional skills, promote the preservation of the Inuit culture, increase youth confidence and leadership and create job opportunities that can keep youth busy while being attached to their cultural roots. The association is

> devoted to supporting the youth of Inukjuak by actively promoting Inuit cultural heritage within the community. The elder's [*sic*] of the community play a major role in the association's activities by passing on their knowledge, providing guidance, story-telling as well as teaching survival skills on the land. Cultural lessons are also held in the association's newly renovated building. Lessons include kayak-making,

qamutik (ski-doo sled) making, harpoon and head making as well as repairs to existing supplies given by hunters to be repaired by a team of elder's [*sic*] and youth to share their knowledge and to close the gap between the generations. (Unaaq Men's Association of Inukjuak, n.d.)

Background

It has only been two generations since Inuit of Nunavik moved from outpost camps to permanent communities that are based on the influences of a modern wage-labour economy. This shift forced Inuit to move away from relying purely on a traditional subsistence living economy toward a mixed economy that incorporates a wage-labour and for-profit model approach to economic and social development. Along with the impacts of colonization, the rapid transition into permanent settlements, residential schools and southern Canadian influences, a for-profit approach to social and economic development in Inuit communities has led to very specific and devastating social issues that have become a part of their reality—child neglect, family violence, alcohol and drug abuse and youth suicide. For Inuit, families are the basic unit of a community and have been the key to their survival in the past—the impacts of rapid modernization have had, for many families, a disorienting effect as the transition was so rapid that many have not had a chance to "catch up" and adjust to the these changes.

Inuit communities also experience a growing imbalance in income within and among communities, creating an unequal distribution of wealth. Some communities are experiencing an economic boom as a result of large-scale development projects (Duhaime et al., 2008), even though only a tiny fraction of the revenue from such projects remains in the local region (Furgal & Prowse, 2008). Most communities lack employment opportunities, income security and adequate education and training opportunities.

In order to understand many of the social problems and challenges facing many Inuit communities in Canada today, it is important to look at the impacts of the historical events that continue to affect Inuit livelihoods. Imposed settlements of early colonization, the rapid transition from living on the land and a traditional economy to living in settlements with the pull of a modern, wage-labour economy, as well as the residential schools experience, have all had major impacts on the livelihoods of Inuit families. Prior to settlement, Inuit lived a semi-nomadic life and communities consisted of small, family-based groupings that travelled seasonally in pursuit of food (Pauktuutit Inuit Women of Canada, 2006). However, throughout the 1950s to the 1970s, the Canadian government forced families to live sedentary lives based in permanent communities that provided "modern amenities" (Egeland et al., 2009, p. 13). The rapid shift from subsistence to a labour economy created "significant disruptions of the traditional culture and values that had guided Inuit for a millennia" (Pauktuutit Inuit Women of Canada, 2006, p. 8). As Inuit communities were being exposed to modern life, the "deterioration of cultural ties to land-base and subsistence activities" began (Furgal & Prowse, 2008, p. 67). Modern life consisted of the introduction of a labour economy and the use of mechanized hunting tools (the rising cost of equipment has also led to a decline in hunting and fishing activities).

Inukjuak is an Inuit community of approximately 1,600 inhabitants, where, according to Statistics Canada in 2006, approximately 1,425 identify as Inuit, of whom 70 per cent are below the age of thirty. Inukjuak is located on the north bank of the Innuksuak River (the east coast of Hudson Bay on the northwest shore of Nunavik). It is known for its turquoise water, turbulent rapids, gentle rolling hills and open spaces that surround the community, which—in the words of local Inuit—"endow the landscape with a silent beauty" (NV of Inukjuak, n.d.). Inuit and other earlier nomadic cultures have inhabited this area for thousands of years (Pituvik Landholding Corporation, n.d.). For the most part, non-Inuit currently living in the community hold various service positions.

Inukjuak, once known as Port Harrison, was the site of fur trade posts maintained by Révillon Frères (1909–1936) and the Hudson's

Bay Company (1920–1958). In 1927, the St. Thomas Anglican mission was founded in the community. The Canadian federal government established a post office and Royal Canadian Mounted Police presence in 1935, a nursing station in 1947 and a school in 1951 (NV of Inukjuak, n.d.). In 1962, the first co-operative store opened and in 1980 Inukjuak was legally established as a municipality (NV of Inukjuak, n.d.). Throughout this period, most Inuit continued to prefer living their traditional lifestyle on the land in at least six large camps distributed along the coast of the current village, visiting the town only to trade. In the 1950s and early 1960s, Inuit began to move to the settlement (Pituvik Landholding Corporation, n.d.).

In 1953, some Inuit families were relocated from Inukjuak to the High Arctic: Qausuittuq (Inuktitut name for Resolute Bay) and Aujuittuq (Inuktitut name for Grise Fiord). Federal officials expressed concern that overpopulation and poor hunting prospects near Inukjuak would lead to an increase in poverty and dependence on welfare (Marcus, 1995). Those who agreed to move were promised a new home where they would be able to hunt many animals, with the added promise that if they were unhappy, they would be transported home after two years. These promises was not kept. Inuit relocatees had to quickly adapt with new hunting techniques in order to survive. From the perspectives of the relocated Inuit, the government had not consulted them on the relocation projects, nor did the government respond at the time to their unhappiness at living far away from family with little to survive on (Elijassialuk, quoted in RCAP, 1992). In 1996, the government of Canada provided monetary compensation to the surviving relocatees and their families and finally apologized to the Inuit in 2010 for broken promises and the hardships they endured.

Another factor that continues to affect Inuit communities, including Inukjuak, has been the rapid increase in southern Canadian influences that immensely impact Inuit youth. Youth are continuously being influenced by southern Canadian values, in turn affecting their level of interest and cultural ties to traditional knowledge and hunting activities. For example, a study found that "younger generation household members were not taking over full-time hunting roles as elders reduce their hunting activity, favouring employment opportunities and other activities" (Ford & Beaumier, 2010, p. 7). A rapidly increasing young Inuit population and a shifting of values are creating problems in the sustainability of Inuit traditional knowledge.

Despite some of the impacts that have been discussed, Inuit continue to be more inclined to traditional work as opposed to wage-labour employment. Given that Inukjuak has only two hundred to three hundred full-time employment opportunities, many community members live on social assistance. Inukjuak also has the highest unemployment rate in Nunavik and therefore community members have a tendency to work at traditional activities since there are very few wage-labour opportunities available. As the majority of the population is under the age of thirty, it is increasingly influenced by nontraditional and more sedentary ways of living (e.g., video games, junk food, television, drinking, drugs, etc.). This phenomenon, compacted with its recent colonial history, has led to the increase of many social ills occurring within the community. For instance, Nunavik's suicide rate for youth between the ages of fifteen and nineteen is forty-six times higher than the rest of Quebec, and for young adults between the ages of twenty and twenty-four, the suicide rate is twenty-three times higher (SIKUnews, 2010).

Unaaq's History

With a high population under the age of thirty (60–70 per cent of the total population), approximately three hundred to four hundred young men live in Inukjuak. The majority of this age group is unemployed and is considered by the Unaaq Men's Association to be an age group at high risk. In 2001, three young men in the community of Inukjuak committed suicide within the same year. The women in the community asked some of the men to find solutions to this increasing social problem and to find ways of supporting young boys and men in the community. This led to the birth of a small men's group that began developing and implementing community projects geared toward youth in the community, working with a small budget averaging approximately $5,000 a year. In 2006, this group was incorporated as the Unaaq Men's Association (Unaaq) and became Nunavik's first men's association. *Unaaq* is the Inuktitut name for harpoon, which is a vital hunting tool used by Inuit men. The use of this term in identifying the association was decided upon by the founding men, who saw themselves as a vital tool in their community in spearheading their goals to actively promote their culture, support their youth and pass on traditional knowledge from the Elders to the youth. There are seven members on the board of directors (including four Elders), who, as a group, decide what activities should be implemented the following year so that funding and project coordinators can be located.

After incorporation, Unaaq was able to hire community members as employees. Today, Unaaq's annual budget averages between $400,000 and $500,000 a year. It works in close collaboration with the Kativik school board (the regional school board) and receives most of its funding from the Ungaluk Program (Safer Communities Program) through Makivik Corporation.[1] This is a crime prevention program that was created by the Quebec government in 2007—delivered by Makivik—as an alternative to building a detention centre in Nunavik for people who commit crimes (Makivik, 2012). This program works through the submission of proposals by regional and community organizations. Other partners include the Kativik regional government, Makivik Corporation, Avataq Cultural Institute and the Nunavik Regional Board of Health and Social Services, among others. Unaaq now has five major buildings, a snowmobile shop and a carpentry shop with major tools used to repair small engines. In 2013, Unaaq intended to seek additional funding sources such as Industry Canada for its recycling program, as well as to increase its annual budget to $800,000 in order to support an increase in activities related to hunting, excursions, kayak making and increased staff.

Human resource costs necessary to run the association are budgeted in each yearly funding proposal. Unaaq receives approximately $300,000 a year for staff to coordinate activities, as well as for hunters, excursion guides and local Elders to act as mentors for local youth. There are presently five full-time employees, three small engine mechanics, and two coordinators (one head coordinator and one assistant). The association also employs part-time employees such as a bookkeeper/administrator, who works 15–20 hours a month, and between six and nine Elder hunting guides who are employed twice a month.

Income varies with responsibilities and experience. For example, directors are paid $200 each month and meet every week or two. Full-time coordinators earn $20–25/hour and full-time mechanics earn $15–20/hour, depending on experience. Elders are paid $30/hour for their services and specialized training. For a full-day hunting excursion, guides are paid $300 for one full day. Youth who participate in the activities may at times receive an allowance of approximately $10 per activity, depending on the importance of the project impact on youth. The level of importance is based on a decision made by the board, with value being placed on survival skills activities. An allowance is also provided when an activity is delivered inside a building—such as the GPS, Mapping & Traditional Navigation course evening activities—so that the association can attract more youth to participate. The GPS Mapping & Traditional Navigation training is aimed at helping youth who become lost on the land when they are hunting; the community feels better when they know their youth can build an igloo for shelter, know where to go and what to do. Therefore, an allowance is provided to encourage youth to "stick to the program" for activities that the association and community feel are important to their well-being.

Activities are free to participants and promoted by the coordinator on the local radio channel—the main medium of announcing information in the community. The coordinator announces the activities, but reaching out to youth and getting them involved continues to be a challenge. Youth are often involved in nontraditional evening activities and the majority of them do not listen to the radio. A solution that is presently being planned is to hire additional coordinators who are within the age range of thirteen and twenty-nine. They are also seeking to add two additional board members who would be within the target age group who would be paid based on a quota of attracting participants. Presently, there are seven board directors: four Elders between the ages of fifty-five and seventy—the pillars and foundation of the association—three men in their mid-thirties and one man in his mid-forties. The addition of two youth on the board of directors and youth coordinators would help Unaaq increase its outreach to their target group. This would also create additional income opportunities within the community for the target age group.

As long as yearly funding is approved, Unaaq helps prevent social ills, keeps youth busy and creates employment within the community. However, obtaining funding can be a challenge at times. For instance, for two summers the association ran out of funding. An application to renew funding had been submitted at a time that was considered late in the season. Therefore, people normally employed had to work without pay for four weeks. However, as soon as the funding was approved, the association paid their staff. This is an example of how having to reapply for funding on a yearly basis can affect the flow of income in a community. A solution to this problem would be for Unaaq to have the opportunity to obtain multiyear funding.

Impact on Community

The Unaaq Men's Association of Inukjuak has developed programs and activities for the community and has been growing over the years. Its goals are to actively promote Inuit culture and create traditional jobs and services, with the overall objective being to support youth within the community. Over the years, the community has witnessed fewer social problems as community members continue to participate in healthy activities together, learn traditional knowledge from Elders and pass this knowledge on to children.

Unaaq welcomes any age and gender group but does focus on teenage boys and young men under the age of thirty. For example, Unaaq provides fox-skinning, sled-making and dogsled-making

5.1 At the Unaaq igloo-building course in February 2012. The igloo was used for Cultural Heritage Week a month later. From closest are Terry Qinuajuak (lifting the block of snow), Noah Echalook and Eliasie Weetaluktuk.
Courtesy of Unaaq Men's Association

lessons for young boys between the ages of thirteen and seventeen. In addition, young women are not excluded if they show an interest in a particular activity. Young women are often interested in participating in ice-fishing excursions and fox-skinning lessons. As mentioned above, the association has had some challenges in attracting interest from this age group. It is often the case that teenagers and young men have their own views influenced by southern Canadian culture, which affects their interest in traditional activities. For example, many prefer to play non-Inuit sports like hockey instead of learning traditional hunting skills. Despite this challenge, Unaaq does take many youth on traditional summer excursions.

A major objective for Unaaq is to support Elders and youth in working closely together through activities and excursions based in Inuit culture. For example, fox-skinning lessons and hunting on the land have been projects where Elders mentor youth. Depending on the season, Elders may take youth out on the land during the weekend. In the winter of 2012, youth and Elders worked together to build a large igloo the size of a small house in front of Unaaq's office (3 m high by 4.5 m wide). During this activity, five Elders were employed to work with middle-aged men and youth to help create snow blocks to build the igloo. Other activities include learning-on-the-land survival skills, dog team training, dealing with emergencies, storytelling, dog sled or snowmobile sled making and making and repairing traditional hunting equipment such as sealskin kayaks.

All of the programs and activities are seasonal, with the exception of the small engine repairs/snowmobile shop, which now operates year-round. Unaaq is most busy in the winter and late fall. In the springtime, when the geese are coming in, the ice is thawing and the lakes are full of fish, it can be difficult to find guides. Even though spring and summer are good times for excursions, it is difficult to attract the necessary people to organize activities since most people prefer to be with their families and engage in their own activities.

In addition to seasonal programs and activities, Unaaq provides year-round space and assistance to local hunters in repairing their small engines. Tools and equipment are made available to anyone who needs to use them. The small engine repairs/snowmobile shop service is a program that started in November 2011 and currently employs three small engine mechanics. The services are in high demand—as of February 2012, the shop had worked on approximately four hundred vehicles since the beginning of the program and generated approximately $4,000 to $5,000 a month based on low cost charges. For instance, a daily cost of $55 is charged for any mechanical services, no matter how much time is required. Elders receive special rates to get their snowmobiles repaired. Mechanics, who are employed on shifts from 9 a.m. to 10 p.m., try to make sure that everything is repaired on the same day. A future component

5.2 Members of Unaaq built a shelter for Elder carvers at Sungaujarnaq (Green Soapstone) in June 2012. From left: Dania Ohaituk, Tommy Niviaxie, Eliasie Weetaluktuk, Juani Ningiuk and Pauloosie Weetaluktuk.
Courtesy of Unaaq Men's Association

intended for this program will be to provide basic tool training, emergency repairs training and basic engine repair and maintenance training for local hunters and youth who are interested in learning these skills.

In 2012, there were also plans to provide recycling services to the community. This program is intended to salvage and gather old/spare parts that are scattered at the local dump. Recycled parts range from bodies, bolts, wheels and spare engine parts, as well as scrap metal and wood. These parts will go toward building an inventory for local mechanics to use for repairs. This will not only help the local municipality manage their dump site by reducing the volume of trash but also provide community members with free or very cheap replacement parts. Instead of buying new and expensive parts from southern Canada, community members can begin with the local inventory. At the start of the program, one full-time position will be created with the view to adding another. This program will be available most of the year, but this depends on the participation of community members, since Unaaq will depend on the generation and retrieval of waste to be able to offer a constant inventory of recyclables. Other projects that were in the planning stages in 2012 included a video documentary of Elders' biographies and a toy manufacturing program to supply daycare centres and elementary schools in Nunavik and beyond.

The community is very supportive of Unaaq as it is a nonprofit association; it creates employment, supports youth and actively promotes the Inuit culture in the community. The municipality is also very supportive and has donated two buildings (one in 2004 and another in 2012), which is of great help to Unaaq in its efforts to create a healthier community. All of these opportunities, whether full-time or part-time, help create employment within the community and provide work experience to the unemployed. For a population of approximately 1,600 inhabitants, there are only two hundred to three hundred full-time jobs in the community while the rest of the workforce is on social assistance. Therefore, any job that can be created and attached to the community member's cultural heritage is an asset not only to the individual but to the community as well.

This association has been bringing the culture alive and keeping it strong within the community of Inukjuak. The dedicated board of directors is on the radio every other week promoting activities and creating new jobs and new projects. Elders are just as dedicated and are seen as role models in the community. It has been said that their humbleness and hardworking nature rubs off on other community members. The association is continuously trying new things to keep Inuit in the community busy and attached to their cultural heritage.

Obstacles

For every success there are always some challenges, but for Unaaq, the successes often outweigh the challenges. As for many other social economy organizations in Canada's North, a long-term challenge for Unaaq is obtaining funding. There are concerns about funding prospects after a main source of funding runs out. For example, Makivik's Ungaluk (Safer Communities Program) funding started in 2007 and continues for twenty-five years. Therefore, Unaaq will need to find other funding sources in order to keep other programs, activities and services alive in the community. The association sees this as a long-term challenge, but they are actively seeking new sources of funding. The main short-term challenge is related to human resource capacity and retention. Ensuring that all positions are properly filled, whether it is a board director or a staff member, could be a challenge. For example, if a current staff member left the association, it would not be an easy task to find a replacement with the necessary background. Despite these challenges, people continuously become interested in the association.

Finally, there is the ongoing challenge of attracting youth to activities that are aimed at bringing them together with Elders to ensure that traditional knowledge is passed on to future generations. Storytelling continues within the community through the radio. However, as mentioned previously, most youth do not seem to be interested in listening to the radio. Therefore, Unaaq continues to try and bridge this gap by providing year-round activities that are not repetitive—and always trying something new—with the intention of attracting more youth.

Conclusion

Unaaq is the first men's association in Nunavik and it would like to see other Inuit communities start their own men's groups in order to support the well-being of youth and employ their Elders. Unaaq would also like to help communities in other regions so that they can share experiences and create healthier Inuit communities throughout

Canada. The association has been supporting other communities in creating their own men's associations and sees itself as a role model for other communities.

Recently, Unaaq has been receiving calls from other communities in Nunavik that are interested in starting and/or maintaining a men's association. For example, the community of Salluit contacted Unaaq to learn how to start and incorporate an association, where to obtain funding and to learn basic budgeting. Kakivak Men's Association in the community of Salluit is based on a similar model to Unaaq in that it provides support to local youth, creates traditional jobs and provides services while actively promoting Inuit cultural heritage. Other communities such as Umiujaq and Kangirsuk have also shown interest in creating their own men's association. They are presently in the idea stage and have been in communication with Unaaq. Unaaq will continue to support communities where it can through the sharing of its experience. Once similar organizations are established, Unaaq would like to have annual general meetings among regions in order to share experiences and see how they can work together. An inter-regional meeting would allow different Inuit community men's associations to come together to share, collaborate and communicate their plans, activities and best practices. For example, such a meeting would allow different communities and regions to exchange hunting practices, traditional practices and compare how kayaks are made. An inter-regional meeting would also provide an opportunity to discuss social challenges and how different communities fight those challenges and help youth stay away from social problems.

The association also intends to promote its organization at a national level. For example, Unaaq intends to send an unfinished kayak to the next Northern Lights trade show and finish building it during the event as a way of promoting the association.[2] It also intends to have other promotional media to raise funds and promote the organization nationally.

The impacts of colonization, the rapid transition of families into permanent communities, the High Arctic relocation, residential schools and the promotion of southern lifestyles all continue to have negative side effects on the socio-economic and mental well-being of Inuit families and communities. Despite this, the maintenance of traditional knowledge and the relationship with the land continue to be of vital importance to ensuring healthy Inuit communities. The Unaaq Men's Association of Inukjuak is a perfect example of how a social economy organization can have a culturally relevant and positive social and economic impact on its community. Unaaq's 2011 annual report explains

> the goals of supporting the youth are being achieved with the collaboration of the municipality, Kativik School Board, Kativik Regional Government, Avataq and other partners. It is important to keep these activities going in the community to actively promote Inuit culture and create traditional jobs in a community with very high unemployment and limited support from outside sources. Social problems are becoming less of a factor compared to years past, thanks to the association and its funding partners. The association very much appreciates the support of the funding sponsors and will keep working hard to expand and create more services for the youth of the community. (Unaaq Men's Association of Inukjuak, 2011)

Author's Note

Most of the information on the Unaaq Men's Association was provided and reviewed by Tommy Palliser, board member and treasurer for the association. Tommy is responsible for ensuring that funding is in place for the association, as well as for the development of funding proposals, annual reports and finding new funding sources. The information was retrieved through a phone conversation, emails, the association's website and reports.

Notes

1. Makivik is a corporation that was created and mandated "to protect the rights, interests and financial compensation provided by the 1975 James Bay and Northern Quebec Agreement, the first comprehensive Inuit land claim in Canada, and the more recent offshore Nunavik Inuit Land Claim Agreement that came into effect in 2008" (http://www.makivik.org/).
2. Northern Lights is an event that was established to create stronger business partnerships between northern and southern Canadian regions and organizations, while also promoting the abundant talent of Canada's arts and culture industry. This event attracts over 140 exhibitors and more than one thousand delegates (Baffin Regional Chamber of Commerce, 2012).

References

Baffin Regional Chamber of Commerce. (2012). *Northern Lights business and cultural showcase of the Eastern Arctic and North returning to Ottawa*. Retrieved from http://www.baffinchamber.ca/node/81

Duhaime, G., Dewailly, E., Halley, P., Furgal, C., Bernard, N., Godmaire, A.,… Grondin, J. (2008). Sustainable food security in the Canadian Arctic. An integrated synthesis and action plan. In G. Duhaime & N. Bernard (Eds.), *Arctic food security* (pp. 73–103). Edmonton, AB: CCI Press, University of Alberta and CIÉRA, Université Laval.

Egeland, G.M., Charbonneau-Roberts, G., Kuluguqtuq, J., Kilabuk, J., Okalik, L., Soueida, R., & Kuhnlein, H.V. (2009). Back to the future: Using traditional food and knowledge to promote a healthy future among Inuit. In Food and Agriculture Organization of the United Nations Centre for Indigenous Peoples' Nutrition and Environment (Ed.), *Indigenous peoples' food systems: The many dimensions of culture diversity and environment for nutrition and health* (pp. 9–22). Rome, Italy: Food and Agriculture Organization of the United Nations.

Elijassialuk, S. (1992). Royal Commission on Aboriginal Peoples. Transcripts, Volume 27 (Inukjuak, QC, 8 June 1992). *Our Legacy.* Retrieved from http://scaa.sk.ca/ourlegacy/

Ford, J.D., & Beaumier, M. (2010). Feeding the family during times of stress: Experience and determinants of food insecurity in an Inuit community. *The Geographical Journal*, 1–18.

Furgal, C., & Prowse, T.D. (2008). Chapter 3: Northern Canada. In D.S. Lemmen, F.J. Warren, J. Lacroix, & E. Bush (Eds.), *From impacts to adaptation: Canada in a changing climate 2007* (pp. 57–118). Ottawa, ON: Government of Canada.

Makivik. (2012). *Ungaluk program (safer communities)*. Retrieved from http://www.makivik.org/building-nunavik/ungaluk-program-safer-communities/

Marcus, A.R. (1995). *Relocating Eden: The image and politics of Inuit exile in the Canadian Arctic*. Lebanon, NH: University Press of New England.

NV of Inukjuak. (n.d.). About Us. Retrieved from http://www.nvinukjuak.ca/en/index_eng.htm

Pauktuutit Inuit Women of Canada. (2006). *The Inuit way: A guide to Inuit culture*. Ottawa, ON: Library Collection of the Geological Survey of Canada.

Pituvik Landholding Corporation. (n.d.). Community. Retrieved from http://www.pituvik.com/Community.html
SIKUnews. (2010, June 7). Nunavik gets more for health, social services. Retrieved from http://www.sikunews.com/News/Canada-Nunavik/Nunavik-gets-more-more-for-health,-social-services-7775
Smiler, S. (2000, April 21). Inukjuak: From outpost camp to modern town. *Special to Nunatsiaq News*. Retrieved from http://www.nunatsiaqonline.ca/archives/nunavut000430/nvt20421_14.html
Southcott, C., Walker, V., Wilman, J., Spavor, C., & MacKenzie, K. (2010, October). *The social economy and Nunavut: Barriers and opportunities* (Social Economy Research Network of Northern Canada Research Report Series RR#1-2010). Retrieved from http://yukonresearch.yukoncollege.yk.ca/frontier/files/sernnoca/PortraitureReportforNunavutv.pdf
Statistics Canada. (2006). 2006 Community Profile for Inukjuaq village nordique. Ottawa: Statistics Canada. Retrieved from http://www12.statcan.ca/census-recensement/2006/dp-pd/prof/92-591/index.cfm?Lang=E
Unaaq Men's Association of Inukjuak. (n.d.). *Welcome to the website of the Unaaq Men's Association of Inukjuak*. Retrieved from http://www.unaaq.org/intro.htm
Unaaq Men's Association of Inukjuak. (2011). *Annual report*. Retrieved from http://www.unaaqmen.org/images/Docs/annual_report_web.pdf

6

Jennifer Alsop

The Naujat Co-operative

History and Impact upon the Community of Repulse Bay, Nunavut

Over its forty-seven-year history, the Naujat Co-operative in Repulse Bay, Nunavut, has seen its fair share of challenges, growth and success. It all began in the basement of the community's Catholic mission in the late 1960s, primarily as a means for local people to sell carvings, furs and fish. Over the past decade or so, it has found ways to become more responsive to community needs, to grow and to reinvest success in co-operative members and the community at large. The co-op is now involved in a variety of aspects within the local economy, including handicrafts, cable service, construction and tourism, as well as grocery and hardware retail sales. The Naujat Co-op's recent success is due to strong management, an engaged and educated board of directors, strong support for the co-operative model within the community and its ability to respond to community needs while retaining standards of financial management.

6.1 Welcome sign for the Municipality of Naujat on the Arctic Circle.
Courtesy of Jennifer Alsop

History

In pre-contact times, Repulse Bay was a meeting and trading place. Each successive group of explorers, whalers, missionaries, fur traders and government officials had a profound impact on the lives of the people who traditionally lived in and around Repulse Bay. Ukkusiksalik, Aivilik and Netsilik Inuit, originally from the Wager Bay area, were drawn to Repulse Bay, starting at the beginning of the twentieth century, primarily for economic reasons (Pelly, 1996). They found work with Scottish whalers and traded furs with both the Hudson's Bay Company and Révillon Frères (Remie, 1983). A whaling station was established in Repulse Bay in 1903, and a Hudson's Bay Company post arrived in 1923 (Bond, 1970). Beginning in the 1950s, the federal government introduced social welfare, schools and other southern institutions across the Arctic. Permanent federally provided housing—the earliest "matchbox" type—was built in Repulse Bay in 1964.[1]

Federal northern policy discussions at the time were dichotomously focused on the "depressed" informal traditional hunting economy on the one hand, and rapid industrial development on the other (Clancy, 1987, p. 191). Beginning in the early 1950s, a third co-operative alternative was proposed as an alternative or supplement to the prevailing centrally planned federal approach to northern socio-economic development (Treude, 1972). The co-operatives were introduced in a centrally planned way; during 1959 to the early 1970s, federal government officials introduced the idea of co-operatives to northern communities, providing financial support in the form of seed money to communities where interest was expressed. While federal public servants, such as Don Snowden and Alexander Sprudz, played a role in setting up several of the first co-operatives, it was often local priests and RCMP officers who were responsible for introducing the idea to recently settled communities such as Repulse Bay.[2]

In Repulse Bay, Gjoa Haven and Kugaaruk (formally known as Pelly Bay), Catholic Oblate missionaries championed the co-operative cause. The dedication of these Oblate missionaries to the foundation of the co-operative model in the North, and principles of mutual support and sharing, is evident in the way in which these co-operatives have grown and developed over the past sixty years (Missionary Oblates of Mary Immaculate, 2009). Father Theophile Didier OMI (1910–1986), an Oblate missionary who spoke Inuktitut, served the Repulse Bay mission on and off from 1947 to 1977. He is well known for his efforts in translating the Bible into Inuktituk.[3] Didier probably had a role to play in supporting the development of the co-operative in Repulse through his role with the Catholic mission in the late 1960s—the period of time in which the co-operative began. The co-op began in the basement of the Catholic mission, as an alternative place and means for local people to sell their carvings, furs and fish. The Naujat Co-op was incorporated in 1968. Donat Milortok, former mayor of Repulse Bay, was the first member (D. Milortok, personal communication, 2009). Later on, when the church tragically caught fire and burnt to the ground, the co-operative was forced to find another space in which to operate, and it began using a small, recently abandoned matchbox house. Soon thereafter, it used a warehouse as the co-op building. After that, it moved to the basement of the co-op hotel until it moved into the current building (D. Milortok, personal communication, 2009). With each successive move, the co-op grew and expanded its activities.

The Naujat Co-op's establishment in the late 1960s signalled the beginning of a new way of "doing business" in Repulse Bay, in which community members were encouraged to participate in the actual operations of the co-operative by contributing to the decision-making process regarding the future direction of the organization. Services offered at the Naujat Co-op have changed throughout the decades after its inception up to the current day. For example, in 1974, the services offered by the co-op included the retail store, carvings, furs, domestic fishing and contracting. In 1989, it offered retail services, a hotel and arts and crafts. In 2009, the list of services had grown to include retail, hotel, cable, fuel distribution, big-ticket property rentals (Yamaha), other rentals, freight contracts, the Nunavut Power Corporation contract, Hunters and Trappers Association Nunavut and calling cards (NWT Co-operative Association, 1975; Arctic Co-operatives Limited, 1989, 2009).

The late 1970s and early 1980s were a difficult time for the co-operative system in the North. Many community co-ops were deemed "not in good standing" due to the state of their finances at the time. The system was challenged on a number of fronts. Notably, the recession of the late 1970s meant that credit was in short supply. Northern co-operatives, such as Naujat, in the 1970s were unable to access financing arrangements through the commercial banks because they had few assets they could use to leverage loans and lines of credit. The Naujat Co-op was significantly affected by the challenging economic climate. As is evident in Figure 6.2, a membership drive was enacted in the early 1980s as a method of income generation for Naujat. In addition, employees were laid off with the hope of being able to do more with less. From 1979 to 1983, and again in 1986, the Naujat Co-op was listed by the NWT

6.2 Membership and Employment, Naujat Co-op, 1975–1986
(NWT Co-operative Association, 1975–1983; Arctic Co-operatives, 1984, 1986)

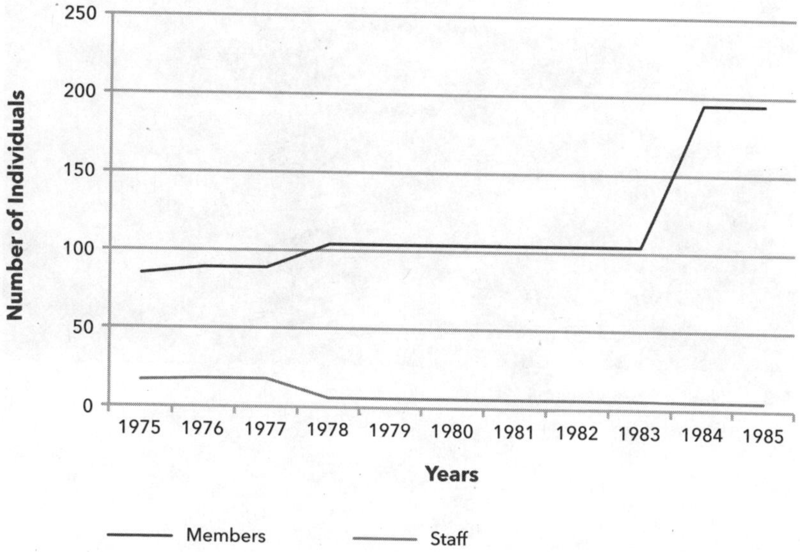

Co-operative Association's annual financial statement as "not in good standing" (NWT Co-operative Association, 1975–1987). The co-op in Repulse Bay struggled to keep its operations afloat until the mid-eighties when an important development within the system provided needed capital to the Naujat Co-op and other northern co-operatives.[4]

Beginning with the establishment of the first Inuit Co-operative at George River, Nunavik, in 1959, up until the early 1980s, financing for co-operatives was made available to those that needed it through the Eskimo Loan Fund (Iglauer-Day, 2000) from the federal Department of Indian Affairs and Northern Development (now Aboriginal Affairs and Northern Development Canada). However, the federal government slowly rescinded this type of economic development funding for Northwest Territories co-operatives due in part to pressure from the business community to cease government financing of community co-operatives (Clancy, 1996).

6.3 Naujat Co-op facility.
Courtesy of Jennifer Alsop

In the mid-eighties, the manner in which co-operatives were financed in the Northwest Territories changed drastically with the creation of the Arctic Co-operative Development Fund (ACDF). ACDF is a self-managed fund of pooled financial resources, owned and controlled by the co-operative businesses receiving funding (Arctic Co-operative Development Fund, 2007). The fund received a one-time subsidy of source capital equalling $10 million dollars in 1986 through financing from Indian and Northern Affairs Canada and the government of the Northwest Territories. ACDF had a tremendous stabilizing effect on the entire system of northern co-operatives, as individual community co-ops financed their expansion plans through a self-renewing fund, which was internal to the system and no longer government-dependent. Despite the financial difficulties the Naujat Co-op endured during the early eighties, it survived and thrived. With organizational reform and a new sense of economic stability, the board of directors and management worked together to create a viable and expanding business through which co-op members directly benefitted from any development and expansion created therein.

Impact on Community

The community, board of directors and management of the Naujat Co-operative have worked extremely hard to ensure the organization's success, as evidenced by developments within the community over the past fourteen years. Members note that unlike its competitor, the for-profit chain Northern Store, the Naujat Co-operative works for its members, providing services and products not generally considered profitable by corporations (Naujat Co-op board members, personal communication, 2009). These services, such as the purchase of local handicrafts, provision of cable, training of staff and construction workers, are provided primarily because they are wanted by the community and they aid more than simply the bottom line of the organization.

The Naujat Co-operative is a large contributor to the local economy. Retail is the largest aspect of Naujat's operations, with the lion's share attributable to grocery sales (Naujat Co-operative, 2008). The goal of the retail operations, as cited by co-op management (J. Kauffman, personal communication, 2009), is to work to reduce the cost of living by providing goods and services to community members at affordable prices. The main issue that members approach board members about is the selection and quantity of merchandise sold at the store (Naujat Co-op board members, personal communication, 2009). Naujat expanded its storage facilities in 2004 and completed construction of a new retail facility in 2012.

The co-op has played a prominent role in community facilities construction. From 2004 to 2009, the Naujat Co-op constructed a Parks Canada facility for Ukkusiksalik National Park (a fourplex owned by the co-op and rented out to staff members), as well as a three- and fiveplex for the territorial housing corporation that provides social housing in the community.

The Naujat Co-op also acts as the de facto bank in town. Management at Naujat cash cheques, process income support cheques for grocery credit and extend credit on grocery and other items, when required. The quality of this service is largely at the discretion of the manager and depends upon his/her relationship

6.4 Inside the Naujat Co-operative store.
Courtesy of Mary Nirlungayuk

with community members. The current manager at the Naujat Co-op knows community members quite well and has been there for the better part of a decade. He knows who is a good credit risk and who is not. It is essentially through informal relationships with co-op members that the manager negotiates store credit (J. Kauffman, personal communication, 2009).

The co-op helps stimulate the local economy by purchasing a variety of carvings from artisans in town. Carvings are purchased by the co-op as needed to replenish supplies for sale. There are times when supplies are high and carvings are not purchased. The co-op provides the only venue in which to purchase local carvings from local carvers, whose numbers were estimated at approximately thirty by the economic development officer (Steve Kopak, personal communication, August 2009). A portion of the carvings produced by artisans in town is sold through Canadian Arctic Producers (Canadian Arctic Producers, 2012), the wholesale art marketing arm of Arctic Co-operatives Limited.[5] Remaining art pieces are on display in the co-op restaurant and are frequently purchased by visiting bureaucrats, construction workers and tourists.

The co-op-owned Inns North Hotel is the only hotel in town. It is a thirteen-room hotel with cable, wireless Internet and a restaurant. The hotel adds a much-needed element to Repulse Bay's economy. Notably, it provides full-time employment to a few individuals and added $62,094 and $79,912 to the local economy in wages in 2007 and 2008, respectively (Naujat Co-operative, 2008).

Finally, Arctic Co-operatives Limited provides a number of educational and training programs to member co-ops such as Naujat. The training manager at Arctic Co-operatives in Winnipeg is responsible for working with co-ops to address training needs for their staff, job training for retail management and support in securing funding for wage subsidies. There is "regional training" for employees. This entails mainly four- to five-day training courses for mechanical technicians, cable technicians, kitchen staff and fuel product delivery drivers. Arctic Co-operatives offers training on the job, which is focused on the training of potential assistant and general managers. Additionally, training was recently developed by Arctic Co-operatives to assist with the professional development of boards of directors and includes a variety of topics focused on leadership skills, human resources and finances.[6]

Reasons for Success and Potential Obstacles

Arctic Co-operatives is one of Canada's most successful co-operative ventures, and possibly the most successful co-operative venture owned entirely by Aboriginal people. Individually, some co-operatives within the system have been more successful than others. In fact, in recent years, a number of communities in the Western Arctic have opted out of the co-operative system in favour of different means of community development. The relative success of co-operatives in general—much like corporations or any other organization of people united in a common goal—is dependent upon the strengths of the relationships among people in the organization; bad management and poor governance can detrimentally impact the co-ops' performance and future operations.

The co-op system is very much a part of the social economy in Repulse Bay. While its structures are well defined and developed, unlike perhaps other elements of the social economy, the system tries to promote commitment, engagement and cooperation within communities and between communities, regions and headquarters. On the other hand, Naujat is a business that must accommodate the needs of its various members with flexible budgets, deadlines, limitations and risk.

The Naujat Co-op is the third-largest employer in Repulse Bay, behind the hamlet and Tusarvik School. Notably, other economic development initiatives focusing on small, individually owned businesses have failed, due in part to the extremely close-knit family relationships that make up the community—essentially, no one wants to go into business with the prospect of making money by selling services to family members. The co-op provides an alternative. Yet a similar principle prevails in its operations, too: external managers generally find more success than those internal to the community. Employees of the co-op do not want to be put in the position of having to say no to a family member in need (J. Kauffman, personal communication, 2009). Strong management of the co-operative at Repulse is a key element of its success.

In the past, Naujat was heavily indebted through loans received from ACDF. Today, the success of Naujat can largely be seen by: a) the degree of community loyalty to the co-op; b) the high level of patronage allocations to members; and c) development and expansion plans. Importantly, the Arctic Co-operatives Ltd. system has not received major inputs of government money since 1986, when the Arctic Co-operative Development Fund was set up to support the financing needs of community co-operatives. While community co-operatives are a major employer in the North, their contribution to the social and economic well-being of northern communities extends beyond positively impacting Aboriginal employment statistics. These democratically run organizations allow community members the opportunity to, at least in part, direct the economic development of their community.

Inuit have long needed to rely upon their extended families and neighbours in order to survive in extremely harsh environmental conditions. Fracture, miscommunication and disagreements could do well to weaken the viability of the community's survival. Where the co-ops have found success, they have provided the means by which anyone within the community can become directly involved in economic decision making. This opportunity is provided to co-op members without their having to make great individual sacrifices to provide a service or economic opportunity to the community. Community co-ops spread financial risk around the community. The advent of Arctic Co-operatives and availability of financing through ACDF throughout the Northwest Territories and Nunavut have meant that when met with challenging economic times, one individual, or community, is not made to carry the entire burden of misfortune. At the same time, in periods of success, wealth is spread around to everyone with a stake in the welfare of the organization through patronage allocations.

The role of co-ops in the North has partly been that of a conduit or bridge by which old social and economic patterns are blended with the wage economy and modern society. The initiation of co-operative policy in the Arctic in the 1960s was primarily a southern construct. However, its early introduction to northern communities allowed individuals to learn of the system in which they were becoming a part. This transition necessarily required a good amount of informal education—on either side—of community members who welcomed a new and inclusive method of economic participation into their communities, and of Arctic Co-operative administrators, who worked to find ways to make the system responsive and sensitive to the needs of communities while also growing and changing in often times dicey external economic conditions. Ensuring a responsive system of administration and available financing that respects the need for community control over decision making is important in ensuring continued growth and development of community co-operatives within the system in the years ahead.

Conclusion

Compared to the traditional business model offered by both Révillon Frères and the Hudson's Bay Company, the introduction of the co-operative way of doing business in the North has created a situation whereby Repulse Bay community members have the opportunity to participate in the operations and economic decision making of a business owned by and for the people of the community. The Naujat Co-op's success over the past decade is due to strong management, an engaged and educated board of directors, strong support for the co-operative model within the community and its ability to respond to community needs while retaining standards of financial management. These successes are reflected by the high degree of community loyalty to the co-op, the high level of patronage allocations to members and its ongoing development and expansion plans.

Notes

1. Up until these permanent homes were built, residents of Repulse Bay lived in tents and shacks that had been built along the shoreline.
2. For more information on the "co-operative approach in the north," please see Sprudz (1977), Mitchell (1996) and Stager (1982).
3. Information about the Oblates who served the mission from 1933 was retrieved from http://www.arcticomi.ca/2repulse.html.
4. Members of the NWT Co-operative Association—individual community co-operatives such as Naujat—provided the state of their financial accounts to the association yearly, which would then publish an annual state of affairs report. Finances were tracked this way up to the mid-eighties and the creation of Arctic Co-operatives Limited.

5. In 2007, Naujat Co-op sold $170,719 worth of local products (3.54 per cent of revenue), and in 2008 it sold $134,814 worth of local products (2.37 per cent of revenue) (Naujat Co-operative, 2008).
6. This training was funded by the Co-operative Development Initiative, a program "designed to help people develop co-ops and to research and test innovative ways of using the co-operative model" (see http://www.coop.gc.ca/COOP/display-afficher.do?id=1232543849777&lang=eng).

References

Arctic Co-operative Development Fund. (2007). *2006–2007 ACDF financial statement*. Winnipeg, MB: Author.

Arctic Co-operatives Limited. (1989). *1988–1989 annual report*. Winnipeg, MB: Author.

Arctic Co-operatives Limited. (2009). *2008–2009 annual report*. Winnipeg, MB: Author.

Bond, E. (1970). *Repulse Bay*. Winnipeg, MB: The Winnipeg Art Gallery.

Canadian Arctic Producers. (2012). *About us*. Retrieved from http://www.canadianarcticproducers.com/About-Us.aspx

Clancy, P. (1987). The making of Eskimo policy in Canada 1952–1962: The life and times of the Eskimo Affairs Committee. *Arctic, 40*(3), 191–197.

Clancy, P. (1996). *Contours of the modern state in the territorial north: Policies, institutions and philosophies*. Halifax, NS: St. Francis Xavier University.

Iglauer-Day, E. (2000). *Inuit journey: The co-operative adventure in Canada's North*. Garden Bay, BC: Harbour Publishing.

Missionary Oblates of Mary Immaculate in the Diocese of Churchill Hudson Bay. (2009). *Repulse Bay—Our Lady of the Snows*. Retrieved from http://www.arcticomi.ca/2repulse.html

Mitchell, M. (1996). *From talking chiefs to a Native corporate elite: The birth of class and nationalism among Canadian Inuit*. Montreal, QC: McGill-Queen's University Press.

Naujat Co-operative. (2008). *Audited financial statement, 2007–2008*. Repulse Bay, NU: Author.

NWT Co-operative Association. (1975). *1974–1975 annual report*. Yellowknife, NT: Author.

NWT Co-operative Association. (1975–1987). *Annual reports, 1975–1986*. Yellowknife, NT: Author.

Pelly, D. (1996). *Wager Bay oral history project: Final report of the history of Ukkusiksalik*. Yellowknife, NT: Parks Canada.

Rea, K.J. (1968). *The political economy of the Canadian North: A interpretation of the course of development in the northern territories of Canada to the early 1960s*. Toronto, ON: University of Toronto Press.

Remie, C.H.W. (1983). Culture change and religious continuity among the Arviligjuarmiut of Pelly Bay, NWT, 1935–1963. *Etudes/Inuit/Studies, 7*, 53–77.

Sprudz, A. (1978). Co-operative development: The project approach—Canadian experience. *Review of International Co-operation, 71*(3), 177–185.

Stager, J. (1982). *An evaluation study of the federated co-operatives in Nouveau Quebec and the NWT after the co-operative development program*. Ottawa, ON: Indian and Northern Affairs.

Treude, E. (1972). Co-operatives in the Canadian Arctic. *Polar Research*, *XLII*(2), 4.

7

Noor Johnson

Ilisaqsivik Society of Clyde River, Nunavut

The Ilisaqsivik Society is a health, wellness and community development organization based in Clyde River, Nunavut, a growing hamlet of around one thousand people on northern Baffin Island. Ilisaqsivik means "a place to recognize oneself" in Inuktitut and is grounded in a philosophical approach that views health, wellness and community development as intertwined, and its programmatic diversity reflects this vision. Founded in 1996, Ilisaqsivik has grown significantly over the past decades; in 2014, the organization raised $3.6 million to run programs serving community members across the entire life spectrum, from prenatal women to seniors. Ilisaqsivik has been awarded several prominent national awards, including the Kaiser Foundation National Mental Health & Addictions Award (2010), the Tides Canada Top Ten award, recognizing Canada's most innovative social enterprises (2011), and the Prime Minister's Volunteer Award for social innovation (2012). This chapter describes some of the programs and institutional innovations that have contributed to Ilisaqsivik's growth and success

7.1 Clyde River, NU, 2012.
Courtesy of Sheba Films and SERNNoCa

as an Inuit-led, community-based organization. It also explores some of the challenges, specifically those related to fundraising and staff capacity, that Ilisaqsivik is currently working to address. The range and quality of Ilisaqsivik's programs and its ability to translate across cultural and institutional norms, values and practices speak to the organization's strength as a model for social economy organizations across northern Canada and beyond.

History of Ilisaqsivik

Like all small communities in Nunavut, Clyde River struggles with a number of infrastructural deficits, including access to health care, employment and mental health services, and a waiting list for government subsidized housing measured in years. Soon after its formation in 1999, the Nunavut government decentralized government services to ten communities across the territory. The goal was to make government, and government jobs, more accessible to the communities. Clyde River was not one of the ten chosen communities, however, resulting in fewer job opportunities and less small business development than in many other Nunavut communities. In addition to these infrastructural challenges, Clyde River residents are working to address and heal the legacies of past government policies, including residential schools, tuberculosis hospitalizations and southern-based educational models, which separated Inuit from their families, from life on the land and from their language and traditions.

In 1996, a group of community members came together to found an organization that would allow Clyde River to develop according to its own vision, bridging economic development and healing and cultural activities. In 1997, the Ilisaqsivik Society was incorporated as a nonprofit, community-based organization with charitable status. With support from the government of the Northwest Territories and the hamlet of Clyde River, the Ilisaqsivik Family Resource Centre was established in the community's former health centre building.

Since its founding, Ilisaqsivik has proven to be remarkably flexible and adaptive both in terms of the programs it offers as well as in the development of new institutional capacities. For example, in 2005, Ilisaqsivik supported the establishment of the Ittaq Heritage and Research Centre (known as Ittaq), an organization dedicated to Inuit leadership of heritage and research activities in the community and surrounding areas. In 2006, Ilisaqsivik purchased a building next door to its family resource centre to house the new Ittaq Heritage and Research Centre, which houses a media production facility. Future plans include an exhibit space, a research library, an archive for oral history and artifacts and facilities for visiting researchers. In 2011, Ilisaqsivik initiated its newest institutional innovation, a project called Tukumaaq, Inc., to help meet its long-term funding needs.

"A Place for Everyone": Ilisaqsivik's Organizational Impact

One of Ilisaqsivik's goals is to be a "place for everyone," creating a comfortable, safe and welcoming environment at its community resource centre and developing innovative programs that meet a wide variety of needs and engage diverse, cross-generational interests. The following programmatic themes illustrate the range of initiatives that Ilisaqsivik has undertaken.

PROVIDING ACCESS TO THE LAND AND *INUIT QAUJIMAJATUQANGIT* (INUIT KNOWLEDGE)

In Inuit culture, concepts of personhood have traditionally been linked to the land and the community, which has been termed an "eco-centric" view of the self (Stairs & Wenzel, 1992; Kirmayer, Fletcher, & Watt, 2009). Modelling these insights, Ilisaqsivik's programs integrate *Inuit Qaujimajatuqangit* (Inuit knowledge—abbreviated *IQ*) and Inuit values into health and wellness education and support services. Working closely with Elders and active hunters, Ilisaqsivik runs land-based programs and *IQ* workshops throughout the year. For example, every summer it runs a two-week healing and wellness camp, attended by up to one hundred people, that combines healing workshops on a variety of topics (e.g., residential schools, the killing of Inuit dogs, drug and alcohol abuse) with *IQ* workshops (e.g., cleaning and preparing skins, medicinal plants). In the winter, the *Ataata/Irniq* (Father/Son) program pairs experienced hunters with male youth, many of whom rarely get to travel on the land, for a two-week trip to fish and hunt seal and caribou.

Another program, *Qimmivut* (Our Dogs), brings youth on a two- to three-week dogsledding trip during which mentors teach them about the traditional role of sled dogs in Inuit culture through hands-on experience in caring for and working with them. In addition to teaching specific skills (e.g., hunting, working with dogs, way-finding, sea ice safety), these trips also provide opportunities for Inuit men and youth to build stronger ties and to support each other in a context that affirms the importance of hands-on work and traditional male roles while also acknowledging the impact of social change on men's relationships to work and family. Inuit men, in particular, have seen their roles in the family and community change significantly over the past fifty years. While they previously were the primary food providers, a role integral to tying families together through sharing networks, this role has been eroded due to the influx of store-bought foods and the increasing importance of wage labour (Collings, 1997).

Ilisaqsivik's *IQ* programs also focus on women's skills and knowledge. Many workshops address seal and caribou skin preparation

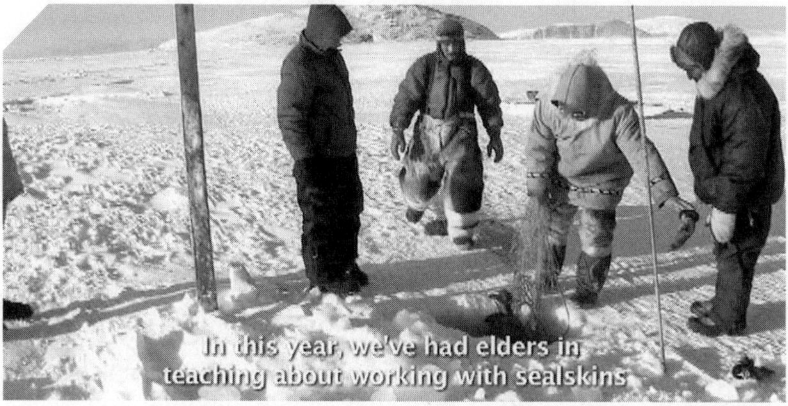

7.2 Elders demonstrate how to work with sealskins, teaching students survival skills as well as Inuit culture, 2012.
Courtesy of Sheba Films and SERNNoCa

and sewing traditional clothing such as parkas, *kamiks* (skin boots) and mitts. Traditional knowledge about childbirth and childrearing is built into programming for parents of young children and pregnant moms-to-be. In 2010, the Arnait (Women's) project, an initiative led by women from Clyde River and nearby Qikiqtarjuaq, along with two female researchers, held an intergenerational berry-picking retreat that focused on building support networks among women while documenting the impact of social and environmental changes on their lives (Dowsley, Gearheard, Johnson, & Inksetter, 2010).

Drawing on its many successes in land-based and *IQ* programming, in 2009, Ilisaqsivik worked with a number of community members to develop and write a proposal to the government of Nunavut, proposing Clyde River as the host community for Nunavut's new territorial cultural school. After a review process that included visiting one of Ilisaqsivik's on-the-land programs, the government selected Clyde River to be the cultural school's location. In 2011, Piqqusilirivik welcomed its first class, comprised of individuals from communities across the territory. Since then, Piqqusilirivik has worked with Ilisaqsivik to coordinate instructors and equipment for a number of land programs.

SUPPORTING HEALTHY FOODS AND HEALTHY LIFESTYLES

Many of Ilisaqsivik's programs provide access to health information, recreation and healthy foods. For example, programs for new and expecting mothers, young parents and preschool-age children combine healthy snacks and meals with information about a range of health issues from the benefits of breastfeeding to diabetes awareness to fetal alcohol spectrum disorders. Ilisaqsivik serves healthy food to over a quarter of the community on a daily basis—around four hundred people per day participate in programs that provide healthy food.[1] These include programs like the school breakfast program, prenatal nutrition, preschool, parents and tots, after-school program, Inuktitut literacy and youth drop-in. Ilisaqsivik sponsors country food programs, sending hunters out about four times a year to bring back fresh seal, caribou and fish and serving the food at community feasts, distributing food to households and in their programs for Elders, children and new and expecting mothers.

PROVIDING COUNSELLING AND DEALING WITH CRISIS AND TRAUMA

Ilisaqsivik's counselling programs combine the strengths of southern[2] and other counselling approaches with Inuit traditions, knowledge and skills, which integrate the individual into the context of family and community (Wihak & Merali, 2003). The organization takes a pragmatic, flexible, client-centred approach that tries to meet the specific needs and interests of the individual seeking counselling. For example, some community members prefer counselling in Inuktitut, while others prefer to speak English. Some request counselling from an Elder, while others may specifically request counselling that does not draw on Inuit traditional approaches and prefer a younger counsellor. If a request is made for an outside perspective, Ilisaqsivik matches individuals with counsellors from other communities, many of whom have gone through Ilisaqsivik's counselling training program. A final, integral part of Ilisaqsivik's counselling philosophy is that it tries to offer opportunities for people to receive counselling outside the office. This can occur in sewing groups, during a walk around the community or out on the land, berry picking or hunting.

Ilisaqsivik's counselling program is set up to enable a quick response to family and community crises. One of the most critical crisis responses is dealing with the aftermath of suicide. During this difficult time for family members, and for the community as a whole, Ilisaqsivik's counsellors immediately coordinate among themselves to provide support to family and friends of the victim, responding in the middle of the night if needed. Ilisaqsivik's community-based counselling model is based on the identification of "natural counsellors"—individuals who family and friends gravitate toward in a crisis. Participating in counselling training often helps these individuals feel more confident in their roles. The training also lends legitimacy, which enables others to recognize who they can approach when they need support.

Overall, Ilisaqsivik's counselling philosophy is based on the idea that the client should lead the process, that different approaches can be useful in different cases and that, for Inuit, it is often effective to conduct counselling on the land when possible. In partnership with Terry Garchinski, a trained therapist who runs Life Works Counselling and Training Services based outside of Calgary, Alberta, Ilisaqsivik developed a two-year training curriculum and handbook entitled, *Our Life's Journey: The Inuit Counsellors' Training and Mentorship Manual* (Garchinski, 2011), which it offers regionally to individuals from communities across Nunavut through workshops and training. Through its training program, Ilisaqsivik has developed a network of on-call counsellors spread across the Qikiqtani region of Nunavut.[3]

BUILDING SKILLS THROUGH HIP HOP AND NEW MEDIA

In addition to its more traditionally focused wellness and *IQ* initiatives, Ilisaqsivik has also excelled at developing innovative programming to help youth and young adults learn new skills that reflect the integration of Inuit communities into the global information economy. In 2006, through a partnership with Ottawa-based Blueprint for Life, Ilisaqsivik began to engage youth through hip hop, leading an initiative that would expand in the following years across Nunavut. The program emphasized physical fitness, drug and alcohol avoidance and peer support, and offered Clyde River's youth a fun, recreational activity and the chance to travel to participate in competitions in Ottawa and across Nunavut.

Another growing initiative focuses on film and new media training and services. In 2009 and 2010, Ilisaqsivik hosted television and media training programs for Nunavummiut youth from across the territory. Participants wrote their own health public service announcements (PSAs), which were broadcast on the national Aboriginal People's Television Network (APTN) and on Nunavut regional television programming. Ilisaqsivik now employs a full-time media coordinator and markets its media services to outside groups, leading to new sources of revenue for the organization and job opportunities for residents. It has produced commercials and PSAs for companies and government agencies, such as an alcohol harm reduction campaign for the government of Nunavut's Department of Health. In 2010, and again in 2014, it was contracted to create the Inuktitut voice-over for a popular APTN children's television show, *Wapos Bay*. The project involved casting Clyde River residents as the show's characters and hiring Elders as language consultants. Ilisaqsivik also did the voice-over for the *Wapos Bay* full-length movie. And in 2014, Mike Jaypoody, the organization's first media coordinator, who learned his skills through Ilisaqsivik programming and leadership opportunities, won the Best Documentary Film award at the Yellowknife Film Festival. His film, *Tony: Back from the Brink*, tells the story of Tony's transformation from addiction and years in jail to becoming a father and a counsellor at Ilisaqsivik.

Building Capacities for Community Development: Translation, Participation and Sustainability

Ilisaqsivik's programmatic variety can be viewed as a sign of its success at implementing the vision of its founders: to enable the community to pursue its own vision and agenda for community development. In this section, I discuss some of the specific capacities that have supported Ilisaqsivik's success, in particular, its role as a cultural translator through grant writing and supporting land-based practices, and its participatory institutional structure. I then briefly discuss several sustainability challenges (financial and staff capacity) that Ilisaqsivik is working to address.

TRANSLATION

One of the essential roles of social organizations is to raise the money required to run programs and pay staff, matching community needs with funding opportunities from organizations and government agencies. Fundraising requires the ability to translate between local priorities and goals and the norms of bureaucratic government agencies that administer grant money. Executive Director Jakob Gearheard raises the majority of the funding that Ilisaqsivik needs through grant writing, a skill set he has mastered through years of community development work not only in Clyde River but also in South America. Working with staff members to help them develop grant-writing skills is part of a strategy for long-term sustainability. These skills are difficult to master at the community level, however, since this kind of translation requires a strong understanding of how bureaucracies work, as well as the current funding priorities that are often based on top-down rather than bottom-up trends. This could potentially be addressed by sending an employee out of Clyde River for advanced training, for example to enroll in a university or nonprofit management course in grant writing. Another approach may be to recruit employees who have spent time working outside of Clyde River in government jobs and are looking for ways to return to the community.

Ilisaqsivik is involved in another form of translation through its support for land-based knowledge through employment. The organization hires Elders and hunters to pass on land skills and procure country food for programs and community feasts, and pays boat, snowmobile and ATV owners to transport people and equipment for land-based programming. Ilisaqsivik isn't the only institution that supports these kinds of activities; the local K-12 school, the Canadian Rangers,[4] the Piqqusilirivik cultural school and, to a limited extent, researchers, sport hunters and tourists also pay community members for their land-based knowledge. In a randomized survey conducted with sixty Clyde River community members in 2010, more than half of respondents (n = 35) reported having received payment for sharing land-based knowledge in the previous year.[5] The money received from these activities, while not sufficient to support a full-time hunter, supplements income from wage labour and welfare, enabling hunting and food-sharing practices to continue. As such, Ilisaqsivik is among a growing number of institutions that translate between two value systems, capitalist wage labour and local kinship networks, helping support the continuation of the latter in the context of the growing influence of the former in Inuit communities.

The interweaving of capitalism and local systems of value, which are based on kinship and food sharing, is not a new phenomenon in Inuit communities. Francis Abele (2009) locates the origins of the "mixed economy," in which Inuit households combine several sources of income and subsistence for their livelihoods, in the introduction of the fur trade and, later, the introduction of cash, credit and wage employment. Nicole Gombay (2010) refers to these arrangements as the "vernacular economy." Direct payment to hunters and Elders for sharing their knowledge and expertise, however, is a more recent development. Payment for knowledge reflects the efforts of communities and Inuit organizations to advocate for the "value" of Inuit knowledge as both an important source of information about the Arctic environment, as well as for the transmission of Inuit culture and identity. While helping support land-based practices, payment for knowledge also creates new forms of interaction among community members. For example, Ilisaqsivik's father-son land trips match adult and Elder hunters with younger men who are often unrelated to their mentors. Without these institutionally created opportunities, some of these younger men would not have the chance to travel on the land, since in most instances hunters only travel with friends

7.3 Ilisaqsivik Society programs in Clyde River take people out on the land to teach survival skills and Inuit culture, 2012.
Courtesy of Sheba Films and SERNNoCa

and family members, and not all Clyde River youth have a relative or close friend who is an active hunter. In interviews, many participants in Ilisaqsivik's land trips emphasized ways in which travel on the land with Ilisaqsivik was different from when they went with family. In particular, they noted the structured nature of Ilisaqsivik's trips compared with less structured family outings. Ilisaqsivik's land trips and the practice of paying hunters and Elders support the transmission of knowledge while also supporting new social configurations and new structures through which knowledge is shared.

While paying hunters and Elders for their knowledge offers a much needed revenue stream that assists with the continuation of these land-based practices, it also changes the way that local people perceive the value of these skills in the context of the capitalist, wage-based economy. Under such a system, local knowledge becomes, at least in some cases, commodified. As Gombay (2010) demonstrated in her book on selling country food in Nunavik, however, Inuit are capable of participating in multiple economies and value systems at the same time. Given the example illustrating how new forms of relationships emerge from paying hunters for their knowledge, it seems important to distinguish among the different contexts in which knowledge is shared. The commodification of knowledge in an institutionalized context does not mean that all knowledge sharing has become commodified; rather, the income generated from these contexts may support the free exchange of knowledge among kinship networks that remain central to Inuit family and community life.

PARTICIPATION

Natan Obed, director of social and cultural development for Nunavut Tunngavik, Inc., the Nunavut land claims organization, described the level of interaction between Ilisaqsivik and the community as "a best practice model that we'd like to see replicated across the territory" (personal communication, August 10, 2010). As with any community-based institution, participation depends on a variety of factors, including the degree to which programming reflects community member needs and interests. Ilisaqsivik's programming is determined by its board of directors, which is comprised entirely of community members. Elder, youth and children's programming areas each have their own committees that meet on a monthly basis. Community representatives offer curriculum suggestions, particularly in areas of Inuktitut language and Inuit culture, and serve as resources for staff members.

Ilisaqsivik's strong focus on health and healing may, however, present an obstacle to engaging certain community members. Jake Gearheard, Ilisaqsivik's executive director, believes that the "healing" discourse can be alienating to some people in the community, particularly men, who might prefer, for example, to "just go hunting" rather than participate in healing workshops on the land. At the same time, the number of community members who attend the summer healing camp has grown steadily as people have become familiar with Ilisaqsivik's balance of healing, wellness and *IQ* workshops. Jake has noted a stronger emphasis on economic development and job skills from Ilisaqsivik board members in recent years, and programs like hip hop and film and new media have engaged more youth. This suggests that programmatic adaptability, including balancing healing and development initiatives, will continue to be important to Ilisaqsivik's participatory approach.

SUSTAINABILITY

Northern organizations are much more restricted in fundraising possibilities than their counterparts in southern Canada because of the general lack of both a corporate presence in the North and a philanthropic base of donors with money to invest in social enterprises. Reliance on government grants presents a particular challenge: usually, only a small proportion of these funding streams can be dedicated to administrative and infrastructural costs such as salaries, building maintenance, heat, office equipment and electricity. Executive Director Jake Gearheard occasionally gets calls from groups in other Nunavut communities who want tips on how to start similar programs, noting: "Their final question is always something like: 'how do you pay for electricity?'" (personal communication, September 10, 2010). When he describes the effort of constantly balancing program grants to find money for salaries and infrastructure, many groups he speaks with decide not to take on the risk of social enterprise start-up.

In 2011, Ilisaqsivik initiated a new business arm called Tukumaaq, Inc. ("a place where you store valuable items") to help meet its long-term funding needs. Tukumaaq's first project was to build a hotel in Clyde River, Naujaaraaluit (a local landmark/place name that means "many seagulls"), which opened in 2015. The hotel has created several new jobs and job-training opportunities, and once it becomes profitable after several years of operations, it will generate a revenue stream that Ilisaqsivik will be able to dedicate to core funding. It also expands much-needed accommodation options for visitors to the community; the only other hotel in town was often fully booked for months, and sometimes years, in advance. This impacted basic service provision for the fly-in community, as health care professionals and government workers all need to stay overnight (Ducharme, 2014). Ilisaqsivik's development of Tukumaaq reflects a wider trend in "social enterprise" to add profit-making enterprises into a nonprofit model; as long as profits are reinvested in the nonprofit, it maintains its charity status. In fact, one of the definitions of "social enterprise" organizations is that they use earned revenue to further social causes (Social Enterprise Alliance, 2011).

An additional sustainability challenge relates to staff development and continuity. Because of the project-based nature of Ilisaqsivik's funding, only a few employees are considered to be full-time, permanent staff members. The others are hired on a particular grant, laid off and then rehired when a new grant comes in, resulting in a relatively high rate of staff turnover (although often the same employees return in the same, similar or new roles). This reflects a wider trend in northern organizations; a 2005 Statistics Canada survey, for example, noted that "social economy organizations in the territories were most likely to report problems related to organizational capacity" compared to similar organizations in the provinces. In particular, organizations struggled with providing staff training and development and finding the right staff members to meet organizational needs (Southcott & Walker, 2009, p. 21).

Ilisaqsivik has made the most of this situation by incorporating job training and skills development into its mission. As one of the largest employers in Clyde River, Ilisaqsivik has gradually formalized its role by developing a professional trainees program to hire, train and promote talent from the community.[6] A series of grants from Kakivak, an organization that supports business development and job training initiatives in Nunavut, has enabled Ilisaqsivik to develop job descriptions and hire new employees for a variety of roles including administration, computer and information systems, early childhood education, film and digital media and librarian positions. As Joelie Sanguya, the Ilisaqsivik board chair, explained, "Many people who have gone through Ilisaqsivik have taken jobs at the school or other places. Once they master what they've started out to do at Ilisaqsivik, then they can get another job" (personal communication, August 16, 2009). In other words, when current or former staff find employment elsewhere, this represents a success for the organization, transforming a challenge into a strength. At the same time, with more core funding and greater staff continuity, the organization would be able to offer better training and support, particularly to management-level staff. In particular, Ilisaqsivik's management and counselling staff would benefit from regular staff retreats and from participating in specialized training programs outside the community. Further research on social enterprises in the North might productively investigate whether organizations with more unrestricted funds have less staff turnover in senior level positions.

Conclusion

Ilisaqsivik strives to be a "place for everyone" in Clyde River, serving the community through a wide diversity of social and cultural programs. Ilisaqsivik's philosophy emphasizes the connection between wellness and community development, enabling the organization to meet diverse community interests and needs. While classical economics views health and individual well-being as an outcome of successful economic development (Sen, 1999), community development approaches have increasingly viewed health as integral to both the means and ends of development (Syme & Ritterman, 2009; Campbell & Jovchelovitch, 2000). Research on First Nations and Inuit communities in Canada also emphasizes the connection between health and wellness and community prosperity (Adelson, 2000; Blaser, 2004).

Ilisaqsivik's broad concept of wellness is matched by flexibility toward concepts of tradition and land-based knowledge, resulting in the innovation of new forms through which land skills can be learned and practised. Equally, Ilisaqsivik has shown itself to be adaptive at the institutional level, supporting the development of the Ittaq Heritage and Research Centre, growing its in-house capacity for film and media production and developing the new Tukumaaq, Inc.

accommodations to generate revenue for the organization. While Ilisaqsivik's programmatic and institutional flexibility and innovation have established the organization as a "best practice model" for Nunavut and beyond, the organization continues to struggle with long-term funding. In particular, restrictions on federal and territorial grants make it difficult to fund salaries and infrastructure. This represents a significant challenge for social sector organizations in the North, and calls for greater flexibility from governments wishing to invest in community-led development and wellness initiatives.

Author's Note

This chapter is based on fieldwork conducted in Clyde River in 2009 and 2010 and follow-up interviews conducted by phone in 2012 and 2015. I am very grateful for the cooperation of the Ilisaqsivik Society and the Ittaq Heritage and Research Centre of Clyde River. I gratefully acknowledge research support from the Social Science and Humanities Research Council and Foreign Affairs and International Trade Canada. I also acknowledge writing support from the Social Economy Research Network of Northern Canada for this case study analysis.

Notes

1. The organization spends around $12,000 a month and an additional $30,000 a year on sealift costs to purchase healthy food for these programs.
2. I use "southern" here to refer to southern Canada; others might refer to these approaches as coming from a Western philosophical and psychological tradition of wellness.
3. As of February 2015, Ilisaqsivik employed five full-time counsellors at its family resource centre (three women and two men, three of whom were Elders). Its network included trained, on-call counsellors. Seventy-nine Nunavut residents had successfully completed at least one or more stages of their counsellor training program, with twenty-seven participants successfully completing the entire program.
4. The Canadian Rangers is a subcomponent of the Canadian Forces Reserve that engages community members in the Arctic and sub-Arctic on patrols for public safety and national security purposes. Participants are paid a stipend for their service. Exercises in Inuit communities incorporate Inuit knowledge about how to survive on the land. See P. Whitney Lackenbauer (2005, 2007).

5. The survey asked respondents to identify whether they had been paid for driving a Ski-Doo or boat, bear monitoring, hunting or taking others out on the land or teaching Inuit knowledge. Survey respondents were randomly selected by having house numbers drawn from a hat. They included equal numbers of men and women (thirty each) across three age groups: 18–34 (twenty total), 35–59 (twenty total) and sixty-plus (twenty total).
6. In 2014, Ilisaqsivik had eight full-time employees, eighty-three half or part-time employees and an additional sixty-eight casual workers.

References

Abele, F. (2009). The state and the northern social economy: Research prospects. *The Northern Review, 30*, 37–56.

Adelson, N. (2000). *Being alive well: Health and the politics of Cree well-being.* Toronto, ON: University of Toronto Press.

Blaser, M. (2004). Life projects: Indigenous peoples' agency and development. In M. Blaser, H.A. Feit, & G. McRae (Eds.), *In the way of development: Indigenous peoples, life projects and globalization* (pp. 26–44). London, UK: Zed Books.

Campbell, C., & Jovchelovitch, S. (2000). Health, community and development: Towards a social psychology of participation. London, UK: LSE Research Online. Retrieved from http://eprints.lse.ac.uk/2587

Collings, P. (1997). Subsistence hunting and wildlife management in the Central Canadian Arctic. *Arctic Anthropology, 34*, 41–56.

Dowsley, M., Gearheard, S., Johnson, N., & Inksetter, J. (2010). Should we turn the tent? Inuit women and climate change. *Études/Inuit/Studies, 34*(1), 151–165.

Ducharme, S. (2015, August 28). New Nunavut hotel will funnel profits into local charity. *Nunatsiaq News Online*. Retrieved from http://www.nunatsiaqonline.ca/stories/article/65674new_nunavut_hotel_will_funnel_profits_into_local_charity/

Garchinski, T. (2011). *Our life's journey: The Inuit counsellors' training and mentorship manual.* Millarville, AB: Bag Man Publications.

Gombay, N. (2010). *Making a living: Place, food, and economy in an Inuit community*. Saskatoon, SK: Purich Publishing.

Kirmayer, L.J., Fletcher, C., & Watt, R. (2009). Locating the eco-centric self: Inuit concepts of mental health and illness. In L.J. Kirmayer & G. Guthrie Valaskakis (Eds.), *Healing traditions: The mental health of Aboriginal peoples in Canada* (pp. 289–314). Vancouver, BC: UBC Press.

Lackenbauer, P.W. (2005–2006, Winter). The Canadian Rangers: A "postmodern" militia that works. *Canadian Military Journal*, 49–60.

Lackenbauer, P.W. (2007). Teaching Canada's Indigenous sovereignty soldiers...and vice versa: Lessons learned from Ranger instructors. *Canadian Army Journal, 10*(2), 66–81.

Sen, A. (1999). *Development as freedom*. Oxford, UK: Oxford University Press.

Social Enterprise Alliance. (2011). What is social enterprise? Retrieved from https://www.se-alliance.org/what-is-social-enterprise

Southcott, C., & Walker, V. (2009). A portrait of the social economy in northern Canada. *The Northern Review, 30*, 13–36.

Stairs, A., & Wenzel, G. (1992). I am I and the environment: Inuit, community, and identity. *Journal of Indigenous Studies, 3*(2), 1–12.

Syme, S.L., & Ritterman, M.L. (2009). The importance of community development for health and well-being. *Community Development Investment Review, Federal Reserve Bank of San Francisco, 5*(3), 1–13.

Wihak, C., & Merali, N. (2003). Culturally sensitive counselling in Nunavut: Implications of Inuit traditional knowledge. *Canadian Journal of Counselling, 37*(4), 243–255.

8

Sheena Kennedy Dalseg

Keeping the Future in Focus

A Case Study of Illiniariuqsarvik Igloolik Head Start

Generally speaking, social economy organizations emerge in response to locally identified challenges and opportunities that arise as a result of social and economic change. The social economy[1] can contribute to community empowerment and citizen engagement through the development of new—and the strengthening of existing—human and social capital. This chapter will offer a case study of one social economy organization that makes such a contribution: Illiniariuqsarvik Igloolik Head Start[2] (Head Start) located in Igloolik, Nunavut.

Igloolik is one of Nunavut's larger communities, with approximately 1,700 residents, located in the Qiqiktani (Baffin) region.[3] Like most northern communities, its population is very young.[4] In 2009, a survey of local businesses and community associations identified twelve social economy organizations in Igloolik, including the co-operative, the hunters and trappers association, three churches,

8.1 Town of Igloolik, 2009.
Courtesy of Sheena Kennedy Dalseg

several local societies and Head Start. That same year, Igloolik's social economy infused over 1.2 million dollars into the local economy in the form of wages, making the sector a significant source of employment in the community.[5]

Illiniariuqsarvik Igloolik Head Start serves as an excellent example of how one relatively small organization can have a significant impact on a community beyond its intended purpose. Not only is Head Start an educational centre for Igloolik's youngest children and their families but in 2011 it employed over thirty residents. The centre was originally created in response to concerns in the community over low levels of attendance among elementary school children. Today, Head Start offers a variety of programs geared primarily at young, preschool-aged children but also offers supports for parents and other caregivers. The staff members are constantly adapting their programs and developing new ones to address current community needs and priorities as they are identified with and by parents and the elementary school.

Perhaps most importantly, Head Start serves as a point of connection in the community for individuals and other organizations. Over the years, Igloolik Head Start has become an important community "hook and hub" (Ball, 2005), bringing together families and other organizations in town, such as the Nunavut Arctic College (NAC), the schools and the health centre.[6] Head Start is considered by the community to be one of Igloolik's most important institutions and one of its greatest assets. As a locally run, culturally oriented family resource and education centre, Head Start represents a long-term vision for Igloolik and its development as a healthy and flourishing community.

Building a Strong Foundation in Igloolik

As mentioned, Igloolik has a very young population, with about one-tenth of its residents under five years of age and just over 40 per cent of the population under fifteen. As is the case elsewhere in Nunavut, children and youth are the focus of many community-planning discussions among residents and local decision makers. There is considerable concern in the community about youth, education and future employment for young people (Hamlet of Igloolik, 2011; Igloolik Community Wellness Planning Group, 2011).

In the early 1990s, a Northwest Territories report indicated that roughly 80 per cent of youth were not completing high school (Allen & MacDonald, 1999, p. 6). In Igloolik, specifically, concerns arose over low levels of attendance in kindergarten classes and the lack of supports in the community to prepare children for school, especially those children with special needs. These reasons, coupled with increasing recognition across Canada that the early years were incredibly important for school-readiness and future success in school and life, led to the creation of the Igloolik Early Intervention Project, as it was then called.

In 1995–1996, the federal government issued a call for proposals across the territories for funding (Community Action Funds) to start up local early intervention programs such as Head Start. At the time, there were a handful of Igloolik residents with teaching and special education experience who wanted to work with parents and local administrators to create such a program for Igloolik. These individuals, with support from the community, including the hamlet and the health centre, answered the call and presented Health Canada with a plan for Igloolik's own preschool program (Allen & MacDonald, 1999; Igloolik Early Intervention Project, 2009b).

Prior to this, there had been some ad hoc projects aimed at preschool-aged children when funding was available, but none had sought to bring all available resources together under one roof. By 1998, after two years of pilot programs, Igloolik Head Start opened its doors full-time. Today, after many years of experience and growth, the centre now offers dozens of programs to Igloolik families (Igloolik Early Intervention Project, 2009b). An early program evaluation of Head Start highlights that following the creation of Nunavut,

> There is an unprecedented potential for social, cultural and personal empowerment in the lives of Inuit families and children. But this positive change cannot happen by itself and requires long-term commitment. Now, in Nunavut, there is (and will continue to be) a growing need for able graduates with the knowledge, skills, and capacity to shape and strengthen our new territory. Inuit are recognizing the need to help children get the best possible start in life, to stay in school, and to become vibrant, productive members of the community throughout their lives. (Allen & MacDonald, 1999)

The recognition of the important role that Head Start plays in contributing to this opportunity continues today.

8.2 Books for the Igloolik Head Start program.
Courtesy of Sheena Kennedy Dalseg

The Roles and Successes of Illiniariuqsarvik Igloolik Head Start

Igloolik Head Start is considered by the community to be one of Igloolik's most important institutions and one of its greatest sources of strength. As an early childhood education and family-focused centre, Head Start represents a long-term vision for the community and its development. The centre strives to offer support to young children and their families, recognizing that a strong foundation is the key to success at the micro (individual) level, as well as at the macro (community) level. The centre takes a holistic approach to community development, building on Igloolik's strengths, which provides a much-needed counterbalance to the vision of economic development tied to major resource extraction projects, a vision upheld by many local and territorial decision makers. This holistic approach is evident in everything the centre does, from the very reasons for its establishment, to the programs it offers, to the way in which and by whom those programs are offered.

What is perhaps most compelling about Head Start is the effect it has had on the whole community. In a relatively small, family-oriented community like Igloolik, the indirect effects of an organization like Head Start can be exceptionally far-reaching and should not be underestimated. Although its primary purpose is to offer preschool programs to children, the centre has become an important educational resource for parents and families, a valuable source of employment and training for women (and, hopefully in the future, for men) and a community hub.

PROVIDING COMMUNITY AND CULTURALLY BASED EDUCATION

Education is at the core of every program and service offered through the centre. The National Committee on Inuit Education's final report, *First Canadians, Canadians First: National Strategy on Inuit Education*, published in the spring of 2011, calls for the development of early childhood education programs, such as those offered by Igloolik Head Start, across Inuit Nunangat. The centre offers daytime programming geared toward children under four years of age, as well as parenting classes (including pre- and post-natal) and infant/toddler classes open to everyone. There are also dozens of evening programs tailored to different groups. Teenaged parents-to-be can receive high school credits for participating in a pre-natal program that offers skills development in the areas of cooking, nutrition and mental health/child development awareness, as well as sewing and traditional parenting practices. The centre has experienced so much growth since it opened its doors that it now offers some programs in other buildings in town because there are more programs than there are time slots and space in the Head Start building.

First Canadians, Canadians First highlights some of the challenges facing Inuit education in Canada, including language, bilingual-bicultural curriculum, parental engagement in education, low attendance and high school completion rates and limited access to post-secondary education. The strategy makes the link between education, employment and broader societal participation, highlighting the importance of investing in the education of young children.

Igloolik Head Start, one of just a few such programs in Nunavut, provides an innovative and community-focused response to some of these challenges. It helps to provide a strong Inuktitut foundation for children and encourages parents to become involved with their children's education from a very young age. Head Start is actively working to achieve community-based and community-focused education. Over the years it has developed ways to fuse Inuit cultural and linguistic educational traditions with southern early childhood education techniques to create a successful community-focused program that is embraced as a local creation.

The preschool programs are aimed at ensuring children develop the skills necessary to succeed in kindergarten and beyond. Head Start allows teachers to assess each child's individual development and to identify learning disabilities or developmental delays early on. The centre reports that all four-year-olds in Igloolik attended Head Start regularly in 2008–2009 (Igloolik Early Intervention Project, 2009a). For those children who do not or cannot attend Head Start, the centre provides an outreach program that includes home visits by centre staff and at-home educational toys and games.

According to parents and staff, one of the centre's greatest strengths is that it is run exclusively in Inuktitut and has a strong focus on Inuit culture. A strong linguistic foundation is seen as essential for success in future work or post-secondary opportunities (Hamlet of Igloolik, 2011). Conventional economic development is focused strongly on job training (that is, vocational and post-secondary school education), whereas the social economy approach embodied by Igloolik Head Start tends to focus on developing and empowering individuals to be active and engaged members of their communities.

EMPLOYING AND EMPOWERING WOMEN

Over the years, the number of people employed at Illiniariuqsarvik Igloolik Head Start has steadily increased with the number of programs offered, particularly in the evenings. In 2010, Head Start had thirty-eight employees—almost exclusively women—most of whom were employed on a part-time basis.[7] Nearly all of the staff members are parents or grandparents of local children. While the more senior positions require a background in education, several of the part-time positions are open to anyone willing to learn. Regardless, most of the women have done some training in early childhood education at NAC (J.-A. Charbonneau, personal communication, November 2011).

The centre's coordinator and senior employees place a strong emphasis on professional development and offer their staff training opportunities whenever funding is available. Head Start staff members have attended courses at the Arctic College, as well as conferences across Canada. They have also been invited to participate in workshops with Elders and teachers in the local schools. In recent years, there have been fewer opportunities for staff to attend conferences or skills development programs, but the hope is that this practice will resume in the future (J.-A. Charbonneau, personal communication, November 2011).

The professional development and on-the-job training that Head Start staff receive means that they are often in high demand for jobs elsewhere, particularly at the elementary school. It is not uncommon for Head Start employees to substitute teach at the elementary school (Hamlet of Igloolik, 2011). In the past, the centre has lost employees to the elementary school because the school is able to offer staff housing, better salaries and benefits. Nonetheless, from a whole-community perspective, this can only be seen as positive.

Head Start is one of a few organizations in Igloolik where local residents can volunteer on a regular basis, and the centre is never short of people willing to help out with various programs or events (C. MacDonald, personal communication, May 2009). Volunteering is one way for individuals to develop new skills and gain work experience. Indeed, many of the part-time employees at Head Start started out as volunteers. Many mothers and grandmothers are able to work or volunteer during the time when their (grand)children are attending the centre's programs.

The women employed at Head Start are empowered through their work and the positive effects are likely to trickle down to their personal lives and families. In an early evaluation report, staff members (all of whom were women) variously said of working at Head Start:

> It gives me stronger confidence in myself and it changes my lifestyle at home and to be a better parent and a positive, friendlier person.
>
> Working here has helped me how to be a better parent by having so many useful resources of parenting and childcare.
>
> I feel much closer to my family. And I feel more important in myself.
>
> I have new ideas, I can communicate better and be less shy. (Allen & MacDonald, 1999, p. 33)

Members of the Head Start staff who participated in a 2010 focus group echoed these statements and expressed that they felt strongly that Head Start was a positive place to work, a place that gave women in Igloolik an opportunity to make an impact in the community, as well as in their own families (Hamlet of Igloolik, 2011).

BRINGING PEOPLE AND ORGANIZATIONS TOGETHER

Head Start is part of a broader network of agencies and organizations in Igloolik that work together toward achieving common goals and objectives, namely self-reliance, community wellness and education. One of Head Start's greatest strengths is that it seeks to share and make use of other local resources before looking elsewhere for support. The organization and its staff make every effort to maintain a positive working relationship with other organizations and agencies in town, particularly the other educational facilities, the health centre and the hamlet government.

There are many examples from Head Start's decade and a half to draw from; however, in the interest of space, two are discussed here.

The first is Head Start's important and long-standing relationship with the community health centre. The health centre and Head Start have worked together to identify and support children with developmental challenges or special needs. Because it has built and maintained trusting relationships with parents over time, Head Start is well placed to encourage families to keep up with doctors' appointments and to provide other supports when needed. Head Start also serves as a liaison between the elementary school and the health centre because of its positive relationship with parents. Further, the fact that nearly every child in Igloolik has attended the Head Start program before kindergarten means that the Head Start staff have an understanding of the home lives of nearly all the children in the community.

Over the years, the centre has also collaborated with Nunavut Arctic College on several occasions to provide practical work experience for NAC students. For example, early childhood education and homecare students are regularly invited to do a practicum at Head Start, and several times over the years students in the trades program at the college have offered their skills to the centre for various projects, including building an on-site kitchen.

Conclusion

Over its life, Head Start has become an important community "hook and hub" for intersectoral collaboration, as well as educational and social and cultural engagement. Many Elders volunteer for the traditional sewing and parenting classes, which provide an opportunity for intergenerational contact and communication (C. MacDonald, personal communication, May 2009; J.-A. Charbonneau, personal communication, November 2011). These evening programs also offer a safe gathering place for women and their children to spend their evenings while learning and developing life skills.

Although it is primarily mothers and their children who spend the most time at the centre, there are many fathers who attend sessions regularly with their families. The Head Start staff is committed to encouraging more male involvement through various programs, such as cooking classes for men and father-children evening sessions.[8] In 2011, a male Elder joined the Head Start team and his primary role was to build traditional Inuit toys. Elders are a valuable part of the Head Start experience for the children and their families; simply by participating in an afternoon's activities, Elders enrich both teaching and learning (particularly language learning).

One of the greatest recognized strengths of the social economy is its flexibility and ability to reflect the socio-economic and cultural context in which it operates. This is certainly the case for Igloolik Head Start. It operates and responds to local priorities in a way that a state-run program would not be able to. In a community where many of the institutions have been implanted from elsewhere, Head Start is quite unique.

The centre was established and continues to be run by Inuit women from Igloolik, which is not only important for the programming it offers but also because it has encouraged widespread community "buy-in." In Igloolik, there is at least one child under five years of age in almost every household. In light of this, it is not insignificant that nearly all three- and four-year-olds in Igloolik attend Head Start regularly. This means, in effect, that Head Start touches nearly every household in the community. It is difficult, if not impossible, to measure the true impact this small organization has had on the hamlet of Igloolik, but it is by all accounts positive and inspiring.

Author's Note

This chapter is based on research I conducted with community partners in Igloolik between May 2009 and September 2010 as part of the *Igloolik Socio-Economic Baseline Study* prepared for the Hamlet of Igloolik (2011) by Frances Abele and myself. Special thanks to Carolyn MacDonald, Iga Kalliraq, Maren Vsetula, Jo-Annie Charbonneau and the Head Start staff members who participated in the focus group for sharing your passion and time with me.

Notes

1. In this chapter, I have relied on the definition of "social economy" laid out by Frances Abele (2009): "the part of the social productive system that lies outside the direct ambit of government programs and large businesses" (p. 38). For more information on the role of the social economy in Canada's northern territories, please see the special issue of *The Northern Review—The Social Economy of Northern Canada* (Spring 2009).
2. Head Start's official name is the Igloolik Early Intervention Project, to distinguish it from being purely an Aboriginal Head Start program. Aboriginal Head Start programs in urban and northern communities are funded by the Public Health Agency of Canada. The Igloolik Early Intervention Project has come to be known simply as Head Start, and so I have used this name here.
3. See Hamlet of Igloolik (2011).
4. In 2009, 43 per cent of the community was under fifteen years of age and the median age was eighteen years. That same year, there were ninety-five infants (aged 0–1) in Igloolik (Hamlet of Igloolik, 2011, p. 13).
5. See Hamlet of Igloolik (2011).
6. This includes medical and social services.
7. This included eleven full-time and twenty-seven part-time staff. There were also many volunteers who spent time at the centre for various programs. Many of these volunteers were Elders and some were teachers at the local schools.
8. Even though the increased participation of men is welcomed and encouraged, Head Start is recognized in the community as a connecting and healing place for mothers.

References

Abele, F. (2009, Spring). The state and the northern economy: Research prospects. *The Northern Review—The Social Economy of Northern Canada*, 37–56.

Allen, K., & MacDonald, C. (1999, July). *Building our strengths together: An evaluation of the Igloolik Early Intervention Project Igloolik, Nunavut* (Unpublished paper).

Ball, J. (2005, March). Early childhood care and development programs as hook and hub for inter-sectoral service delivery in First Nations communities. *Journal of Aboriginal Health, 2*(1), 36–54.

Hamlet of Igloolik. (2011). *2009–2010 Igloolik socio-economic baseline study*, prepared by Sheena Kennedy Dalseg and Frances Abele.

Igloolik Community Wellness Planning Group. (2011, July). *Igloolik community wellness plan*, prepared for the Nunavut Community Wellness Project.

Igloolik Early Intervention Project. (2009a, April). *Aboriginal Head Start renewal report*.

Igloolik Early Intervention Project. (2009b, April). *Head Start program overview*.

National Committee on Inuit Education. (2011, June). *First Canadians, Canadians first: National strategy on Inuit education 2011*. Ottawa, ON: Inuit Tapiriit Kanatami.

9

Julia Christensen

Folk on the Rocks

The Beat That Sustains

Every summer, on the third weekend of July, the rocky shores of Long Lake in Yellowknife, Northwest Territories, resonate like the body of an acoustic guitar. From the main stage at the annual Folk on the Rocks music festival, the sweet sounds of artists like Buffy Sainte-Marie, Leela Gilday, Elisapie Issac and Fred Penner belt forth into the midsummer air. Over the years, the festival weekend has been marked by forest fires, spectacular displays of thunder and lightning, rain, rain and more rain and even a partial eclipse of the sun. Yet nothing has been able to stand in the way of the festival's commitment to promoting the North and celebrating its music. In fact, the festival has grown consistently, year to year, with the main stage now flanked by side stages, a beer garden stage, a cultural area, an artisan marketplace and many delicious food offerings. What's more, it has become a significant part of the local calendar year, a holiday weekend in its own right, with northerners and southerners alike planning their summers around an annual pilgrimage to the sandy site at Long Lake. As attendance has grown, the festival has spread its wings, extending its reach beyond one weekend in July to take an active role in supporting northern music throughout the year. But as the festival has grown, its northern spirit remains the same. True to tradition, since the very first festival weekend in 1980, Folk on the Rocks has drawn to a close late Sunday night (and on more than one occasion, early Monday morning), with a spirited Dene drum dance—festival revellers and performers alike, stepping through the sand to the beat of the skin drums and the song in the drummers' throats, a song that vibrates through the pulse of this place—the North, its lands, its people, its heart.

History

The idea for a music festival in Yellowknife took root in 1978 after Ted Wesley, a local musician, attended Yukon's Farrago Folk Festival in Faro. Inspired by what he had seen and heard, he set out to create a similar festival in Yellowknife. Other locals joined in, and Ted soon had a small team, including his wife Lesley, his sister-in-law Heather Pritchard and his friend Michael Marrapese, to help turn his vision into reality. Rod Russell was recruited to coordinate the festival. Using scrap wood he had scattered around his lot, Rod built the festival's main stage. On June 20 and 21, 1980, on the very site that continues to host the festival to this day, the inaugural Folk on the Rocks festival was held, with approximately 1,500 people in attendance.

In 1987, the festival moved to its now traditional annual time slot—the third weekend in July. Festival organizers had originally labelled themselves the Society for the Encouragement of Northern Talent, a name that speaks to the key original objective of the music festival, but by 1993, the society became known simply as Folk on the Rocks. Despite the change in moniker, the festival's principal mandate to support and encourage northern talent remained the same. Included within this mandate is a commitment to celebrate northern Indigenous peoples and cultures, a pursuit that motivated

9.1 Folk on the Rocks thirtieth anniversary poster, 2010.
Courtesy of Folk on the Rocks

the creation of the festival's cultural area in the early 1990s. Here, festival goers are invited to learn from Indigenous community members and Elders about local history, cultural traditions and what it means to be an Indigenous person in today's North. Over the years, the cultural area has been the site of demonstrations on teepee construction, caribou and fish preparation and tasting, and drumming.

In 1998, the main stage built by Rod Russell in 1980 was finally replaced by a sturdier structure. That same year marked one of the most memorable performances of Mother Nature during the festival weekend: a massive forest fire threatened possible evacuation as water bombers buzzed overhead. On one festival evening, a water bomber dropped down to collect water from Long Lake and then, to a mix of delight and horror on the part of festival goers, seemingly emerged out of nowhere from behind main stage, loaded down with water, appearing to narrowly miss the top of the stage frame in its ascent.

Since that very first Folk on the Rocks weekend in 1980, the festival has consistently brought an impressive lineup of northern and southern performers to its stages each year. The annual festival lineup is guided in part by the festival's efforts to maintain a rough 50/50 split between northern and southern performers. The local/global formula, in combination with the expansion of Folk on the Rocks to include other arts and cultural elements during the festival weekend, has meant that attendance has grown over the years from 1,500 in its inaugural year to over four thousand in 2011. However, as attendance has risen, and the festival has spread its wings, festival organizers are faced with significant questions. Organizers must consider the ultimate capacity of the festival and how to allow for the festival's evolution while, at the same time, respecting the land, its resources and its people, and what they can collectively sustain. After all, not only does the festival site have its limits in terms of its size but it relies heavily on the contributions of local businesses, government and especially volunteers, and the numbers of each are constrained by the small size of the local community. Thus, while the social economy is intrinsic to the success of the festival, in order to maintain that relationship, Folk on the Rocks can only grow as much as its local network of support can handle.

Impact on the Community

Folk on the Rocks' reach extends beyond the city of Yellowknife to embrace the North as a whole. At the same time, by drawing southern performers and festival goers, the festival has had a significant impact both nationally and globally.

However, a great festival requires a solid foundation, and since its humble beginnings, Folk on the Rocks has become an indelible part of the northern cultural and social fabric. Not only does Folk on the Rocks receive the support of northern performers, the festival has become a key point on the yearly calendar, with local volunteers, businesses and governments banding together to ensure the festival's success.

In addition to its cultural and social significance, Folk on the Rocks supports, and is supported by, the local economy in many significant ways. First, the festival provides an open-air arts venue for northern and southern performers, artists, craftspeople and food vendors. The festival also receives a tremendous amount of support from local businesses, which, in turn, benefit from the exposure that such a well-attended festival garners them. As a result of festival efforts, approximately 80 per cent of the budget stays in the North.

Folk on the Rocks' important role in the community extends well beyond the festival weekend. Over the years, the festival has held many other events throughout the rest of the year, such as business workshops for northern performers on career management in the performing arts. The society also organizes other annual musical events in Yellowknife such as the Ice Jam, a musical event that takes place at the Explorer Hotel several months in advance of Folk on the Rocks to both raise funds and promote the festival.

Folk on the Rocks has also organized several different initiatives over the years to connect with people and communities outside of Yellowknife. For example, in 1982, the Folk on the Road program was launched to bring festival performers out to smaller communities in the North. That year, several musicians climbed aboard a bush plane and flew to Whati and Fort Smith to perform, much to the delight of local audiences. Another program, Blues in the School, was launched in the 2000s. In 2011, Blues in the School took place in Inuvik and Hay River in collaboration with the Northern Arts and Cultural Centre (NACC) in Yellowknife.

Folk on the Rocks has played a key role in the career development of many northern performers. This impressive list is too long to provide in full here, but it includes such celebrated artists as Leela Gilday, Jay Gilday, Tanya Tagaq, Digawolf, Lee Mandeville, Aaron "Godson" Hernandez, Pat Braden and Susan Aglugark, to name a few. Moreover, the festival is one of the most important North American music festivals for modern Indigenous music (Diamond, 2007).

9.2 Festival goers dancing at Folk on the Rocks, 2014.
Courtesy of David Whitelock

The festival also has an immeasurable influence on the southern artists who come to perform on Folk on the Rocks stages. For many southern artists, Folk on the Rocks is the reason for their first visit to the North and is their first time experiencing the hospitality, late-setting sun and diverse musical performance traditions of the region. Festival organizers report that several artists have left the festival with new ideas for musical sound and lyrics, based on their experiences in Yellowknife and at the festival. Folk on the Rocks also provides a forum for musical artists who may not otherwise cross paths to explore new collaborations. Some of the most special festival moments over the years have resulted from innovative, eclectic performances from several performers from that year's lineup, each from a different musical tradition, sharing the stage in song.

The Reasons for Success and Barriers to Success

Much of the success of Folk on the Rocks can be traced directly back to the northern community and its ongoing support of the festival, as well as rising interest in northern and Indigenous tourism (Hinch, Hall, & Johnston, 1995). The lure of the North—its landscapes, its light, its people—is a strong pull for visitors to the region (Milne, Grekin, & Woodley, 1998). However, many of the reasons behind the festival's success are also the source of its challenges, an experience common among festivals and other attractions in rural or remote regions (see MacDonald & Jolliffe, 2003). Navigating this delicate balance, and nurturing the opportunities rather than letting the obstacles get the best of them, is a constant struggle for festival organizers.

While Folk on the Rocks is a Yellowknife-based event, the society is wholeheartedly committed to the North—and not just the Canadian North but rather the entire circumpolar region. However, realizing such a vast commitment often proves difficult, as the costs associated with circumpolar travel are immense. Nevertheless, the festival strives each year to include performers from northern regions outside of Canada, such as the Tuvan throat-singing group, Chirgilchin, from Russia, that attended the festivities in 2005. Keeping the lineup fresh is an integral factor behind the festival's success, for it draws festival goers each year with the promise of hearing new music, expanding their understanding of what the North is and what it means to the people who inhabit the circumpolar region.

Festival organizers stress that the program could not run were it not for the many donations of time, funds and other necessary resources. While funding for the arts in Canada is very difficult to obtain, Folk on the Rocks has benefitted tremendously from the in-kind and financial support of local businesses, as well as both territorial (Northwest Territories and Nunavut) and federal governments. The festival also generates earned revenue, largely through ticket sales.

The festival's longevity is also due to the hard work of volunteers. As former Folk on the Rocks executive director, Penny Ruvinsky, has explained, "It is truly our volunteers that make the festival a reality each year. Beginning with the board of directors who work tirelessly over the twelve months leading up to the festival to the 350 volunteers who sign up to actually work the festival" (personal communication, February 2012). Volunteers are especially needed because the paid Folk on the Rocks staff is very small, consisting only of the executive director, who is the only full-time staff member, the artistic director, who is on quarter-time and two to three seasonal staff who are hired from March through to September. One challenge resulting from the festival's reliance on volunteers, however, is the potential for volunteer burnout. This reality is one that the board of directors is very cognizant of and they attempt to cope with this challenge by drawing on volunteers when their help is needed most: immediately before and during the festival weekend. Also, festival organizers make sure to publicly express their thanks to volunteers, acknowledging them by name in the festival program and throwing a volunteer appreciation party once the festival is over. However, the biggest show of thanks is the free festival admission that volunteers receive if they volunteer for the equivalent of one full festival day.

Meanwhile, with the festival's northern location central to its identity and significance, there are also challenges associated with holding such a major event north of 60. The first? Mosquitoes. But as Penny Ruvinsky notes, "We can't do much about that" (personal communication, February 2012). Accommodation is another challenge each year. Even though local hotels provide immense support to the festival by offering discounted or free accommodation, there are only a limited number of hotel rooms available in Yellowknife, and there are no other nearby cities or towns that the festival can rely upon for overflow. The festival makes up for this through the recruitment of local households willing to billet performers. Nevertheless, finding enough beds is a recurring concern.

The high cost of travel to the North is also a huge issue. Flying performers and their equipment to Yellowknife from across the country, let alone the rest of the globe, is extremely expensive. Canadian North Airlines is one of the festival's largest sponsors, which takes a significant strain off the festival's travel budget. However, co-ordinating schedules is often a problem and there are times that organizers have to resort to using other airlines to get performers to and from the city. As a result, approximately 40 per cent of the festival's budget for securing performers is spent on travel. The steep costs associated with travel and accommodations also result in a limited budget left over for performer fees. Folk on the Rocks is a professional festival, hiring professional musicians for its lineup each year. Even still, coming up with the funds to pay performers what they would normally receive is always a challenge and often performers will agree to attend the festival for a much lower fee than they would normally garner. The opportunity to play the Folk on the Rocks stage, meet other musicians and, for southern artists, to experience the North and its hospitality are often seen as a form of compensation by musicians. Regardless, festival organizers often wish they had greater access to funds to pay performers a higher rate.

The sustainability of festival attractions is an ongoing concern among cultural event organizers around the world (Carlsen & Getz, 2006; Choi & Sirakaya, 2006; Getz, 2008). In recent years, Folk on the Rocks organizers have focused on the idea to "right-size" the festival. In other words, to recognize the reality that Yellowknife is a small and relatively isolated community, which poses limits in terms of how much the festival can grow. This has to do not only with the capacity of the festival's Long Lake location (approximately 4,500–5,000 people) but also the limits of accommodation, food venue capacity (both on- and off-site), as well as transportation challenges. All of these factors mean that the festival can only grow to a certain extent and also determine the festival's ability to earn income revenue, which directly impacts the budget. This tight fiscal

9.3 The Strumbellas perform at Folk on the Rocks, 2014.
Courtesy of David Whitelock

and creative balance is something the festival continues to juggle successfully, but nevertheless it is always in flux.

Finally, while the festival receives ongoing support from local businesses and government, one significant challenge that organizers perpetually face relates to the need for a broader acceptance and recognition of the role that the arts play in the social and economic landscapes of the local community, territory and nation. The government's commitment to the arts, or its lack thereof, directly affects the festival and its ability to promote the rich musicality of the North.

Looking Ahead

A look back over the more than thirty years that Folk on the Rocks has been in operation illustrates a consistent upswing in terms of venue quality, outreach and community engagement, performers, attendance and revenue. There have been some significant challenges, such as pulling together the funds needed each year to keep the program going, but the festival's history demonstrates that the commitment of the local business and volunteer communities has gone far in seeing the festival grow from a small community music festival in 1980 into an event that is world-renowned. What's more, Folk on the Rocks is a northern event, with a steadfast pledge to build bridges between performers across the circumpolar North, as well as between northern and southern artists. Not only has the festival played a critical role in recognizing and further developing the vast and diverse cultural landscape of the North, it also provides a special event that is quintessentially northern and one that has demonstrated to community members and visitors alike the richness of the North and its people.

Looking toward the future, the key challenge for Folk on the Rocks will be "right-sizing" the festival and determining how this will guide the look and feel of Folk on the Rocks. The festival also hopes to place an even greater emphasis on supporting collaboration, both on and off the Folk on the Rocks stage, between performers.

Another key priority moving forward is "greening" the festival, a commitment that began several years ago and continues to grow more and more with each passing year. Through a partnership with Ecology North, a green strategy for the festival has been developed that sees new greening initiatives taken on each year. Food vendors are now required to use recycled and compostable dishes and utensils (available locally), and Ecology North is in charge of managing festival recycling and garbage. Folk on the Rocks is also looking at alternative sources of power to minimize the festival's carbon footprint even further. Looking out from the festival's main stage area onto the surrounding landscape of Precambrian Shield, spruce and birch trees and the blue waters of Long Lake, one can easily understand the need to respect what the land can sustain. Through efforts to "right-size" and "green" the festival, we will be dancing through the sand to the beat of Dene drummers for many Folk on the Rocks festivals to come.

Author's Note

Thank you to Penny Ruvinsky for participating in an extensive interview for this chapter.

References

Carlsen, J., & Getz, D. (2006). Strategic planning for a regional wine festival: The Margaret River wine region festival. In J. Carlsen & S. Charters (Eds.), *Global wine tourism: Research, management and marketing* (pp. 209–224). Oxfordshire, UK: Cabi Publishers.

Choi, H.C., & Sirakaya, E. (2006). Sustainability indicators for managing community tourism. *Tourism Management, 27*(6), 1274–1289.

Diamond, B. (2007). The music of modern indigeneity: From identity to alliance studies. *European Meetings in Ethnomusicology, 12*(22), 169–190.

Getz, D. (2008). Event tourism: Definition, evolution, and research. *Tourism Management, 29*(3), 403–428.

Hinch, T.D., Hall, C.M., & Johnston, M.E. (1995). Aboriginal people in the tourism economy of Canada's Northwest Territories. In C.M. Hall & M.E. Johnston (Eds.), *Polar tourism: Tourism in the Arctic and Antarctic regions* (pp. 115–130). Hoboken, NJ: John Wiley & Sons.

MacDonald, R., & Jolliffe, L. (2003). Cultural rural tourism: Evidence from Canada. *Annals of Tourism Research, 30*(2), 307–322.

Milne, S., Grekin, J., & Woodley, S. (1998). Tourism and the construction of place in Canada's Eastern Arctic. In G. Ringer (Ed.), *Destinations: Cultural landscapes of tourism* (pp. 101–120). Oxford, UK: Routledge.

10

Jerald Sabin

Alternatives North

A History

The Northwest Territories' official opposition does not meet during regular sessions of the legislature. Indeed, no such role exists under the territory's model of consensus government. Instead, a self-styled substitute meets every Wednesday at noon in the offices of the Public Service Alliance of Canada (PSAC), on 49th Street in downtown Yellowknife. Representing a progressive coalition of labour, feminist, environmental and ecumenical groups, Alternatives North has emerged as a "consistent and persistent" political voice calling for social and economic justice in the territory.[1] Since 1992, the coalition has offered an alternative vision of political and economic development that often contrasts sharply with that of industry and the government of the Northwest Territories (GNWT). Through its outreach activities, research papers and policy briefs, Alternatives North has shaped political and policy debate, found strong support both inside and outside the legislature and won positive policy outcomes for its supporters and allies.

The success of Alternatives North, however, was not inevitable. Founded just as the Canadian nationalist movement collapsed, the small coalition could have disappeared into obscurity as quickly as its national counterpart following the 1993 federal election, a story I return to below (Ayers, 1998). The survival of Alternatives North is the result of its ability to capitalize on political opportunities in the Northwest Territories (NWT) and its unique organizational structure that stresses collaboration and flexibility. Relying upon a consensus-based model of decision making, the coalition has focused its efforts around three policy areas: social and economic justice; environmental sustainability; and peace. Knitting together its activities is a well-established normative framework that enables the diverse membership of Alternatives North to choose projects and allocate its time and resources.

From the perspective of the social economy, Alternatives North is significant for both analytic and practical reasons. Analytically, any organization that can thrive using consensus decision making and distributed leadership for twenty years is remarkable. Perhaps more exceptional has been the maintenance of working relationships between groups that often interact at cross-purposes in other situations. The cooperation within Alternatives North of women's groups and the Catholic Church, for example, or labour unions and environmentalists is not reflective of current political trends in North America (Mayer, 2009; Rayside, 2011). Practically, Alternatives North demonstrates the capacity of volunteers to produce high-quality research and writing on pressing policy issues. In addition, social economy organizations are important players in contemporary political debate, as Alternatives North illustrates.

This chapter presents the history of this unique northern institution. I argue that Alternatives North's success relates both to its flexible and responsive organizational model, as well as the open political opportunity structure of the Northwest Territories. I begin by outlining the origins of Alternatives North in the Canadian nationalist and anti-free trade movements of the late 1980s and early 1990s, and the evolution of the organization's structure and operation in response to political and economic upheavals in the NWT over the subsequent two decades. I outline several successes, as well as explore the challenges facing the organization, such as the lack of Aboriginal participants and organizational renewal. I conclude with a longer discussion of Alternatives North's significance for northerners, progressives and students of political science.

The Origins of Alternatives North

The contemporary coalition known as Alternatives North was not the first to bear that name in the Northwest Territories. In the mid-1970s, in the wake of the Mackenzie Valley Pipeline Inquiry (Berger Inquiry), non-Aboriginal support groups formed in both southern and northern Canada to advocate for the recognition of Aboriginal rights, land ownership and self-determination (McCullum & McCullum, 1975; Sabin, 1995). Yellowknife's northern support group formed in April 1977, about three weeks before the proposed release of the Berger Inquiry's final report. The group was named Alternatives North in order to provide "an alternative voice on northern issues which relate to Aboriginal Rights" (Alternatives North, 1977a). The sixteen original members met on a Sunday evening at the Wildcat Cafe in Old Town and included figures like Fr. Rene Fumoleau and Lois Little, both of whom would go on to play important activist roles later in the territory's history (Alternatives North, 1977b). The group wrote letters to politicians and national newspapers, and it held workshops in support of Aboriginal rights but also to give voice to "one group of people who have not been adequately heard...in the North who are non-native and who are *opposed* to a Mackenzie Valley Pipeline and related developments" (Redvers, 1977). The group was very active during the summer of 1977, expanding its sphere of activism to include environmental and workers' issues, before petering out in 1978.

The contemporary organization to bear the name Alternatives North held its first meetings in 1992 at the offices of the Northwest Territories Federation of Labour in the Bowling Green Building on

49th Street in Yellowknife. Its founding members were a diverse group representing labour, women, the Catholic Church and environmentalists. This core group of activists included Jim Evoy, president of the Northwest Territories Federation of Labour; Sister Marie Zarowny of the Diocese of Mackenzie-Fort Smith; JoAnne Lowell, a local feminist; Suzette Montreuil, who was a social justice coordinator at the diocese, and Kevin O'Reilly, with an interest in peace and environmental issues and also Montreuil's husband. During its first two years, Alternatives North worked mainly on peace issues, such as the denuclearization of the Arctic, and social justice work, including a submission on northern issues for the Centre for Policy Alternatives' 1994 *Alternative Federal Budget*. They were, as O'Reilly put it, "a lean, mean machine and certainly much smaller than we are now" (personal communication, October 2011). The group's early work was unfocused, however, and this reflected larger patterns in the political environment.

Alternatives North grew out of a national movement for economic and social justice in the late 1980s and early 1990s. This was a period of significant structural change in both territorial and federal politics. In the Northwest Territories, the political class and media were preoccupied with the negotiation of the Nunavut Land Claims Agreement, including a territory-wide plebiscite on the new boundaries of the NWT in May 1992 (Dickerson, 1992; Henderson, 2007). Focus was drawn away from the regular activities of the GNWT and some activists were concerned that policy decisions by the government were not being adequately debated. In addition, the discovery of diamonds in 1990 at Lac de Gras led to the largest staking rush in Canadian history. With the spectre of increased mining on the horizon, the diversion of political attention away from ensuring socially, economically and environmentally sustainable development policy was alarming for social justice advocates. Ben McDonald, an early member, said there was no watchdog in the territory at that time. There was a significant need, he said, "for information on the North, and there was really no one watching the North—the governments and institutions that are operating up here, and so it fell to us to do that" (personal communication, October 2011).

Meanwhile, at the federal level, a loose coalition of labour, environmental and social justice organizations were mobilizing to oppose the North American Free Trade Agreement between Canada, the United States and Mexico.[2] The sector mobilized rapidly in response to the "neo-conservative tenets of the 1980s and 1990s—privatization, downsizing, free trade, deregulation—[that to them] represented ill-conceived, if not ideological, responses to the mounting social and economic problems facing...Canadians" (Ayers, 1998, p. 4). The most prominent representation of this was the Pro-Canada Network (PCN), formed in April 1987 by the Council of Canadians, the Canadian Labour Congress, the National Action Committee on the Status of Women and GATT-fly, an ecumenical economic justice coalition of Canadian churches (Bleyer, 1997).[3] The PCN enjoyed considerable success in the lead-up to the 1988 federal election. However, the election of another Progressive Conservative majority and the loss of its anti-free trade campaign placed the ability of the PCN to "sustain popular mobilization and protests...under severe strain" (Ayers, 1998, p. 117). In the wake of this defeat, national popular sector activists recommitted themselves to a network-structured and coalition-building style of politics and to expanding their activities, resource base and membership moving forward.

Reconstituting the PCN under the name Action-Canada Network (ACN) in 1991, popular sector activists began mobilizing groups across the country to oppose the North American Free Trade Agreement negotiations and, on the domestic front, the Charlottetown Accord (Ayers, 1998; Bleyer, 1997). Through its local contacts at PSAC and the Northwest Territories Federation of Labour, Evoy and Montreuil were encouraged by the ACN to start their own "popular sector" coalition to bring the national movement's work to the territory. Local partners that approached to join the new organization—dubbed "Alternatives North" for its commitment to provide an alternative vision—mirrored the national coalition and followed a similar pattern of development.[4]

National support for this type of coalition building collapsed quickly following the 1993 federal election. As Ayers (1998) argues, "a declining set of political opportunities in the 1990s, prompted in part by the constraints imposed by economic globalization and in part by the election in 1993 of a Liberal Party majority and the electoral and political decline of the federal New Democratic Party... undermined the potential of the popular sector" (p. 6). Alternatives North, however, did not disappear, despite the decline of its national counterpart. Both organizational and environmental factors account for its survival and eventual prominence.

Organizational Structure and Activities

Alternatives North's organizational structure has been key to its longevity as the organization has been able to adapt and react to its changing political environment. Members of the organization downplay the importance of how their organization operates. Aggie Brockman, a member of the coalition since 1996, often says that its members are "remarkably unpreoccupied" with themselves and their group (personal communication, October 2011). Montreuil agrees, stating that

> We've never been a group to write policies about ourselves. If anything, we do have a "policy" to work by consensus or by two-thirds majority. Although, we've never had to vote. Even at the beginning, we didn't have a clear mandate—it was an evolution. The mandate came from proactive activities, and reactions to what government and private industry were doing. Over the last five years, we've tried to make annual goals, but it's really tough with all the new stuff that's going on. (personal communication, July 2009)

Employing a model of consensus decision making and distributed leadership in all of its activities has not been without challenges. Collaboration is applied to all activities, from letter writing to determining the organization's strategic direction.[5]

An example from a fall 2011 meeting illustrates the functionality of Alternatives North's brand of consensus governance. The spread of the nascent Occupy movement to Canadian cities—complete with its economic justice message—captured the attention of group members. Following an acknowledgement of similarly aligned goals with the emerging movement, the assembled members of Alternatives North started to discuss whether they, too, should participate. Beyond concerns over Yellowknife weather in late October, speakers expressed both enthusiasm for the movement, as well as caution over the use of the organization's resources and good reputation to support the controversial movement. One speaker highlighted the irony of "occupying" land that has already been occupied and colonized by non-Indigenous peoples. The ultimate decision was to wait. Perhaps later phases of the movement would require Alternatives North's work. Discussion was free-flowing, with members, both long-time and new, participating. Deferring in this sense was not inaction, or a sign of paralysis stemming from the consensus model, but instead a cautious and rational decision about organizational capacity. With several promising projects underway, it was decided that the membership could afford to wait.

SAMPLE OF MAJOR CAMPAIGNS

Alternatives North engages in research, education and advocacy, all of which have been particularly busy since 2005. Its projects fall into three broad areas: socio-economic justice, environmental and economic sustainability and peace.[6] Alternatives North has produced alternative budgets for the NWT, hosted political debates during federal and territorial elections, held protest marches, sent information mailers to every household in the NWT and engaged in countless letter-writing campaigns. I will highlight two more recent activities below that illustrate the breadth of the organization's activities, as well as its successes.

THE MACKENZIE GAS PROJECT JOINT REVIEW PANEL

The Mackenzie Gas Project (MGP) represented a turning point for Alternatives North. Before 2005, Alternatives North had been an unregistered voluntary organization whose interventions into public policy debates were prepared through volunteer labour. The size of the development and its potential for impacts on the NWT necessitated a different approach by Alternatives North. Intervener funding was available, along with grants from labour unions, to pursue paid research highlighting the human costs of the gas pipeline. Like the Berger Inquiry of the mid-1970s, the Mackenzie Gas Project Joint Review Panel (MGPJRP) represented an opportunity to underscore the social, economic and environmental impact of development on northerners and the Northwest Territories. There was also a concurrent review of the MGP taking place under the National Energy Board. While it did not provide funding, it was also a site of important decision making. Alternatives North felt it could influence both processes by capitalizing on its participation in the MGPJRP.

Alternatives North became a registered society under the Northwest Territories Societies Act in 2005. Over the course of the next three years, it would receive over $100,000 in funds to carry out research related to the MGPJRP. This included a number of in-depth studies, submissions and presentations over a three-year period (Abele, 2007; Parlee, 2007; O'Reilly, 2007). Alternatives North was successful in its bid to have the MGPJRP consider several significant socio-economic factors in its review, and several of its recommendations were adopted in the final report. While the government did not act on those recommendations, Alternatives North nonetheless set the groundwork for future battles over resource development and its implications for the NWT. While the MGP was approved by the National Energy Board in 2011, the project was suspended due to poor market conditions in 2012. In later 2013, a revival of the project was proposed, but as of this writing (early 2016), no significant announcements have been made (Northwest Territories, 2013).

Capitalizing on the success of its advocacy work with the MGPJRP, Alternatives North engaged in other resources-related campaigning. It has taken on the role of "independent oversight" of the Giant Mine Remediation Project by the federal government, which has left over 237,000 tonnes of arsenic trioxide underneath the site and within reach of Yellowknife's water source (O'Reilly, 2012, p. 50). This work has included running oversight workshops and partnering with researchers in studying the long-term health and environmental impact of the Giant Mine site. Alternatives North has also been an active participant in debating the devolution of control over public lands and natural resources to the territorial government. While this devolution occurred in April 2014, the group advocated for greater public participation, including a referendum. Alternatives North has partnered with Yellowknife-based environmental group Ecology North to oppose the dismantling of regional land and water boards in favour of the territory-wide board agreed to by the GNWT, Aboriginal groups and the federal government (Alternatives North, 2014). Finally, the group has been active in opposing the practice of hydraulic fracturing in the territory, or fracking, including calling for a moratorium on the practice in early 2015.

ANTI-POVERTY CAMPAIGN

Alternatives North, along with fourteen other organizations and three municipal governments, began a campaign in late 2010, calling for the development of an anti-poverty strategy by the GNWT.[7] During the 2011 territorial election, Alternatives North sent a one-question survey to all forty-seven candidates across the territory. These surveys are common during elections, but they hold particular importance in a system of consensus government where there are no party platforms to guide voters through candidate preferences. The question read: "If elected, will you start to work immediately with business, community groups and others on an NWT anti-poverty

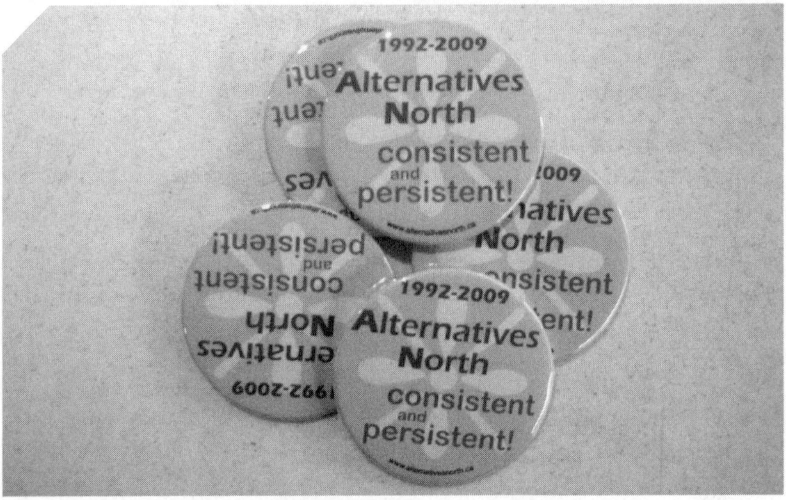

10.1 Alternatives North buttons, 2009.
Courtesy of Jerald Sabin

strategy?" Approximately 70 per cent of candidates responded in the affirmative, while eighteen out of the nineteen (soon-to-be) elected MLAs also responded in the affirmative.

What is remarkable about this campaign was its breadth. For very little money, Alternatives North was able to inform voters of their local candidates' responses through local newspaper advertising and mailers to remote community households. Communications volunteer Craig Yeo argued, "You can really see the democratic possibilities of an organization like Alternatives North in the Northwest Territories. With limited resources and a small organizing team, we were able to reach every household in the territory and make a discernable impact on the campaign" (personal communication, October 2011). The eventual policy outcome of such an effort remains to be seen, although the GNWT did table a report on poverty in February 2012, stating their intention to develop an anti-poverty strategy. This type of campaign is typical of Alternatives North, which has used similar strategies during the MGP campaign, as well as in previous elections.

In June 2013, the GNWT released its anti-poverty strategy, titled *Building on the Strengths of Northerners: A Framework for Action on Poverty*. Alternatives North member Julie Green welcomed the government's framework, recognizing that it did not reflect everything for which the group had advocated and stating that "the completion of the strategy is a step forward, but implementation will be the big test" (Alternatives North, 2013). In its 2015–2016 budget, the GNWT announced significant increases in spending on its anti-poverty programming, bringing total spending on the framework to $12.2 million. To continue its anti-poverty work, Alternatives North spearheaded the creation of another coalition called No Place for Poverty, whose thirty-one members include municipalities, Aboriginal organizations and nonprofit organizations representing environmental, disability, poverty, gender and labour issues.

Challenges

Two significant challenges face Alternatives North. The first is the absence of Aboriginal voices within the organization. There have been few Indigenous participants and no Aboriginal organizations are official coalition members. While alliances occur around specific issues and events between Alternatives North and Aboriginal organizations, these relationships are rarely sustained. Brockman says, "We haven't done enough to reach out to Aboriginal organizations—we have common goals, but it's the execution that is the problem" (personal communication, October 2011). Members want to see this change, but as another leader said, "We deal with the issues of settler society and its institutions. Aboriginal groups have their own battles and issues, and so it would be great if we could work together, but we each have our own work to do" (personal communication, October 2011). Bridging the gap between settler and Aboriginal civil society is a challenge for all voluntary and nonprofit groups, irrespective of their activities. Developing strategic alliances with Aboriginal organizations builds much needed trust and sets the stage for greater collaboration in the future.

Equally pressing is the need for transition planning to ensure the long-term sustainability of the organization. Alternatives North's active membership is primarily middle-aged. This brings considerable experience and knowledge to its activities but without necessarily passing this experience on to a younger generation of activists. While concern over the absence of youth voices has abated in the last five years as a number of young people have joined the group, ensuring a successful future transition at the leadership level remains an issue. Many Alternatives North members cite founding members Montreuil, O'Reilly and McDonald as the "glue" that keeps them together. Their ability to engender trust among the membership is key to both the consensus model and the organization's successful campaigns.

Significance

Alternatives North is a significant northern social economy organization and one whose work and model should be emulated, for several reasons. First, Alternatives North has built a large network of organizations, activists and politicians who are dedicated to social and economic justice for the NWT. As France Benoit, a member since 2006, says, "It's like going to weekly therapy for activists. When the world and your work seem too much—there is too much to do, so much to address—meeting with those people rejuvenates your spirit. You can keep going" (personal communication, October 2011). Alternatives North nurtures its membership and in return receives a high level of dedication and loyalty to the organization and its activities.

The wide array of organizations and individuals that participate in Alternatives North also uses the opportunity to coordinate their work and resources. These groups include the YWCA, the Centre for Northern Families, the Pembina Institute, Focus on Palestine, Ecology North and the Diocese of Mackenzie-Fort Smith, among others. Although it does not formally count many Aboriginal groups in its membership, it often engages in joint activities with such organizations as the Dene Nation.[8] Alternatives North has also made significant inroads into territorial politics at all levels. It counts two members of the legislative assembly among its close allies: Wendy Bisaro, MLA for Frame Lake, and Bob Bromley, the member for Weledeh.[9] It also has allies—or "progressive friends," as one member said—on Yellowknife's city council, including councillors Shelagh Montgomery, Paul Falvo and Amanda Mallon.

Second, Alternatives North is significant for its unique method of organization and work. Maintaining working relationships among the diverse interests listed requires diplomacy and the development of mutual trust. This has happened through the development of a shared normative framework. There are issues that the coalition knows it cannot touch if it wants to survive. As one member put it, "We can't touch something like abortion. Our coalition members couldn't agree on something like that. But with so much other work available to us, we don't even need to go there. This is a useful forum and we know how to use it in a way that gets things done" (personal communication, October 2011). The distributed leadership of Alternatives North has managed this task and gained results.

Finally, Alternatives North is significant because it has changed the political discourse over the past twenty years in the NWT. In doing so, it has also gained policy victories for its membership and constituency. As Brockman says, "We also provide great value for money" (personal communication, October 2011). As much of Alternatives North's work is done on a volunteer basis, the results are that much more valuable.

Conclusion

It seems that the political circumstances that led to the creation of Alternatives North have come full circle. The 2008 global financial crisis and subsequent recession have caused social and political unrest across the Western world. With the rise of the Occupy movement and the stunning electoral performance of the NDP in the 2011 federal election, perhaps coalition and social justice politics are once again on the upswing. Certainly, Alternatives North's social justice agenda seems far more current and in step with happenings in Yukon and Nunavut—as well as southern Canada—than during the economic boom years of the 2000s. The politics of income inequality, social justice and sustainable economic development have returned. Alternatives North has been carrying the torch for the last twenty years and will continue to do so for the foreseeable future.

Author's Note

I would like to thank Frances Abele and Chris Southcott for inviting me to participate in this project and Valoree Walker for her logistical support. I would also like to thank Aggie Brockman, Suzette Montreuil, Kevin O'Reilly, Ben McDonald, Shauna Morgan, France Benoit, Shelagh Montgomery and Craig Yeo for embracing this project. Finally, thank you to David Brock, Amy Groothius and Laurel for their hospitality in Yellowknife, and Kyle Kirkup for his support.

Notes

1. "Consistent and persistent" was the organization's slogan during their twentieth anniversary year in 2012.
2. The "popular sector" describes "a broad cross-section of groups that had struggled through the 1981–2 recession, including trade unions, women's groups, social agencies, Native peoples, and farmers...These groups shared broad characteristics of economic and political marginalization from major decision-making institutions in Canada, including a rank and file that was not drawn from the elite of establishment levels of Canadian society" (Ayers, 1998, p. 4).
3. GATT-fly, reminiscent of "gadfly," was founded in 1973 to oppose the General Agreement on Tariffs and Trade. It was an ecumenical group representing the Anglican, Lutheran, Presbyterian, United and Roman Catholic churches (Bleyer, 1997).
4. The participation of NWT women's groups would come later with the addition of such members as Aggie Brockman, who was on the board of the Yellowknife Women's Centre, and Arlene Hache.
5. Alternatives North employs a list service to communicate with members and among its core group of activists. The Alt-Plan list-serv is used to circulate draft letters, discuss upcoming issues and coordinate responses to events in between meetings. Those who write letters for Alternatives North have their work subjected to several rounds of editing and revision by other group members. Brockman believes this produces higher-quality work: "While it can be difficult

to have your work rewritten, it often leads to something much better than any one of us could do" (personal communication, October 2011).

6. The organization has had a long history in peace activism. While not motivated by English-Canadian nationalism, as national coalition equivalents had been, Alternatives North has nonetheless addressed the pressing peace and international issues facing Canada. In 2003, Alternatives North helped organize protests against the Iraq War.
7. This campaign expanded to include twenty-five groups, four municipalities and the Dene Nation by early 2012.
8. For example, on December 15, 2011, the Dene Nation joined with Alternatives North in calling for MLAs to uphold their commitment to develop an anti-poverty strategy for the territory.
9. Alternatives North members are quick to point out that while not formally associated with the group, these MLAs and coalition members find common cause on a number of social and political issues.

References

Abele, F. (2007). *Education, training, employment, and procurement* (submission to the Joint Review Panel for the Mackenzie Gas Project).

Alternatives North. (1977a). *Alternatives North*. Northwest Territories Archives, Alternatives North Fond, Yellowknife, NT.

Alternatives North. (1977b, April 17). *Meeting Minutes*. Northwest Territories Archives, Alternatives North Fond, Yellowknife, NT.

Alternatives North. (2013, June 6). *GNWT anti-poverty framework a good basis for action*. Retrieved from http://www.alternativesnorth.ca/Portals/0/Documents/Poverty/2013%2006%2006%20Alternatives%20North%20Anti%20Poverty%20Framework%20media%20release.pdf

Alternatives North. (2014). *Alternatives North, Ecology North jointly present opposition to Bill C-15 Part 4*. Retrieved from http://www.alternativesnorth.ca/Portals/0/Documents/Regulatory%20Affairs/MEDIA%20RELEASE%20Alternatives%20North_Ecology%20North%20Jointly%20Present%20Opposition%20to%20Bill%20C15.pdf

Ayers, J.M. (1998). *Defying conventional wisdom: Political movements and popular contentions against North American free trade*. Toronto, ON: University of Toronto Press.

Bleyer, P. (1997). Coalitions of social movements as agencies for social change: The Action Canada Network. In W.K. Carroll (Ed.), *Organizing dissent: Contemporary social movements in theory and practice* (pp. 102–117). Toronto, ON: Garamond Press.

Dickerson, M.O. (1992). *Whose north? Political change, political development, and self-government in the Northwest Territories*. Vancouver, BC: UBC Press.

Henderson, A. (2007). *Nunavut: Rethinking political culture.* Vancouver, BC: UBC Press.

Mayer, B. (2009). Cross-movement coalition formation: Bridging the labour-environment divide. *Sociological Inquiry, 79*(2), 219–239.

McCullum, H., & McCullum, K.T. (1975). *This land is not for sale: Canada's original people and their land*. Toronto, ON: Anglican Book Centre.
Northwest Territories. (2013). "Mackenzie Gas Project." Yellowknife, NT: Department of Energy, Mines, and Resources. Retrieved from http://www.emr.gov.yk.ca/oilandgas/mgp.html
O'Reilly, K. (2007). *A review of selected environmental management issues for the proposed Mackenzie Gas Project* (submission to the Joint Review Panel for the Mackenzie Gas Project).
O'Reilly, K. (2012). Giant Mine, giant legacy. *Northern Public Affairs, 1*(2), 50–53.
Parlee, B. (2007). *A model for monitoring the effects of the Mackenzie Gas Project on health and well-being of communities in the Mackenzie Valley* (submission to the Joint Review Panel for the Mackenzie Gas Project).
Rayside, D. (2011). The Conservative Party of Canada and its religious constituencies. In D. Rayside & C. Wilcox (Eds.), *Faith, politics, and sexual diversity in Canada and the United States* (pp. 279–299). Vancouver, BC: UBC Press.
Redvers, P. (1977, June 8). Letter. Northwest Territories Archives, Alternatives North Fond, Yellowknife, NT.
Sabin, P. (1995). Voices from the hydrocarbon frontier: Canada's Mackenzie Valley Pipeline Inquiry (1974–1977). *Environmental History Review, 19*(1), 17–58.

11

Julia Christensen

From Hockey Sticks to Carrot Sticks at the Top of the World

The Inuvik Community Greenhouse Project

A greenhouse in the land of the midnight sun seems all too fitting, but it wasn't until an old hockey arena was slated for demolition that the idea really "grew." Today, the Inuvik Community Greenhouse is an example of the potential in community innovation and collaboration (Abelson, Giacomini, Lehoux, & Gauvin, 2007). The success of the project also serves as a reminder of the serious food security concerns in Inuvik: garden-fresh produce is hard to come by in the small town of 3,700 on the Mackenzie Delta and, when it is available, it comes at a steep price. Indeed, food security across the Canadian Arctic is a significant concern (Chan et al., 2006; Lambden, Receveur, Marshall, & Kuhnlein, 2006). The Inuvik Community Greenhouse is one step forward in boosting local food security through the engagement of

11.1 The Inuvik Community Greenhouse, housed in a former hockey arena, 2009.
Courtesy of Valoree Walker

local residents in vegetable food production (Dowd, 2008; Fillion et al., 2014). The greenhouse project has also inspired communities across the Canadian North to develop their own community garden and greenhouse projects so that they, too, can harness the energy of the bright Arctic summer nights. The most recent example is the newly minted community greenhouse in Iqaluit, Nunavut (George, 2008).

History

In 1998, the Grollier Hall hockey arena stood empty in the heart of the town, carrying with it the heavy memories of Grollier Hall and its legacy as a residential school (Langston, n.d.). Replaced by a newer facility, the arena was a weighted remnant of a difficult community past. Initial plans were to tear the facility down entirely, but local Ron Morrisson and then Deputy Mayor Peter Clarkson came up with a better solution: turn the old arena into a community greenhouse. While both men already tended their own outdoor garden plots in the summer, they knew that home gardens were hard to maintain in Inuvik for several reasons (Langston, n.d.). Many people in the community live in apartments or row houses with little outdoor space for gardens. For those locals who do have garden space, getting plants to grow well in permafrost is a delicate art. Soil, bedding plants and other garden tools also tend to be expensive in Inuvik, preventing those with limited budgets from participating in their own home gardening. Morrisson and Clarkson envisioned a space that would facilitate northern gardening for the entire community, as well as be a venue for knowledge sharing and community interaction. They also thought that a greenhouse would help to alleviate some of the big challenges associated with northern living: the high cost of fresh produce and reliance on food that travels far distances in order to reach geographically remote northern locations (Mahoney, 2004).

Despite the anticipated benefits of a community greenhouse, many local residents thought a greenhouse project sounded expensive and absurd. Undeterred by naysayers, Morrisson and Clarkson formed the nonprofit Inuvik Community Garden Society and initiated a greenhouse feasibility study as well as a fundraising campaign. The society was soon able to secure financial support from the territorial and federal governments, as well as several local donors. With half a million dollars in hand, the society was ready to begin implementing its greenhouse plans. On a cold, dark day in early January 1999, workers began gutting the old arena and converting its shell into a greenhouse, one sheet of greenhouse plastic at a time.

That summer marked the first growing season of the Inuvik Community Greenhouse and locals clambered to sign up for plots. Soon the greenhouse came to life with tomatoes, lettuce, carrots, basil and more, not to mention all the community members who walked through the door to tend their plots or simply to see what was going on. The growing season lasts from mid-May to early September, and in the middle of the summer there is a distinctly tropical vibe inside; the humidity hangs heavily in the air and you can almost see plants grow before your very eyes in the intense twenty-four-hour sunlight. The facility's main floor houses over eighty garden plots on just over one thousand square metres, tended to by approximately one hundred local gardeners. The second floor,

11.2 Garden boxes inside the greenhouse, 2009.
Courtesy of Valoree Walker

though much smaller at 360 square metres, holds a modest commercial operation. It is here where bedding plants are grown each year and sold to greenhouse gardeners and the general public to support greenhouse revenue. But despite the many local gardeners with greenhouse plots, there is a long waiting list carried over year to year, made up of other locals who would like to gain access to the facility.

The Impact of the Organization on the Community

Many now seasoned green thumbs in the community had never gardened before the greenhouse opened for operation. One of the most profound impacts that the Inuvik Community Greenhouse has had on the local community is exposing it to the joys of gardening. A new knowledge base has been built in Inuvik as a result. While basic gardening is part of this knowledge transmission, community members have also learned to adapt skills and techniques applied in southern gardening contexts to the Arctic, where the sun shines for twenty-four hours a day in high season. What's more, ordering seeds and growing fresh produce has motivated many local gardeners to experiment with fruits and vegetables they had never seen before. One local gardener described growing up in the Inuvik region, believing that fruits and vegetables grew in cans. Christmas oranges were the only fresh fruit she had as a child. Though local grocery stores now carry wide varieties of fruits and vegetables out of the can, gardeners born and raised in the delta are expanding their horizons even further, experimenting with new produce not found at the local store, including kohlrabi, purple carrots, mustard greens and heirloom tomatoes.

Not only is eating a greater diversity of fruits and vegetables good for one's health but the act of gardening is good for the spirit. In the past, Peter Clarkson has even referred to the greenhouse as a "community wellness centre" (Langston, n.d.). Many greenhouse gardeners speak about the therapeutic aspects of gardening—during the summer months, they can escape to a quiet, tropical oasis in the heart of the community and tend plants to their hearts' content. It is also an important site for community building, with many gardeners acknowledging that the greenhouse brings people together who might not otherwise cross paths in their work or day-to-day lives.

Indeed, community outreach and engagement is key to the greenhouse's mandate. The greenhouse is not only for individual gardeners: several community groups maintain plots at the greenhouse, including the Inuvik Food Bank. Additional plots are also set aside for Elders. These efforts at inclusion support a sense of community ownership at the greenhouse and work to ensure the food produced there supports the local social fabric in the broadest way possible.

Not only has the project encouraged the physical health of residents, it has also inspired new ways to care for the local environment. The greenhouse has also motivated new habits in the community. For example, before it opened, few residents composted their kitchen scraps during the year. Now there are bins to collect household compost for use in the greenhouse. Individual households also participate in their own composting, which they then use to start seedlings in the weeks leading up to the start of the growing season.

The greenhouse provides an important educational resource to local residents. Several local teachers have used the greenhouse as a living classroom for their students. Witnessing the growth of new life and learning the skills needed to nurture seedlings into full-grown plants provide important insights that many local school groups have profited from during educational tours of the facility. The Inuvik Youth Centre also has a plot that it uses to educate its youth about growing their own food. Workshops are also held in the greenhouse to teach local gardeners new skills, and workshop space is also provided for other nongardening outreach activities. Other initiatives like canning and food dehydration workshops also help gardeners extend the positive benefits of their gardening into the colder months.

The greenhouse has had a community-wide impact as a draw for new tourists to the region. It has become a mini tourist attraction, motivating travellers to make the long (but beautiful) drive up the Dempster Highway to see the greenhouse under the midnight sun. It also boosts the local economy through the Saturday morning market held weekly during the growing season. The greenhouse is also involved in several town beautification initiatives. Flowers grown by greenhouse gardeners are displayed in local store windows and hung in flowerpots along the main street. Flowers are also purchased from the greenhouse to fill window boxes for social housing units in the community. These small things contribute to community pride and add new elements of colour and freshness to the northern urban landscape.

The reach of the Inuvik Community Greenhouse extends far beyond the town itself. Impressed with the success of the project, and inspired to bring about similar benefits to local community engagement and food security, Nunavut's capital of Iqaluit has recently developed its own community greenhouse program. Buzz about Inuvik's gardening craze has also travelled down the

Mackenzie Valley to Yellowknife, where it has influenced the expansion of Yellowknife's community garden program.

The Reasons for Success and Barriers to Success

Like many of the other social initiatives profiled in this book, the Inuvik Community Greenhouse would not be the success it is today were it not for the contributions of its members. Members pay a small annual fee to use their plots, which varies according to size, but they must also commit to volunteering for at least fifteen hours over the greenhouse season. Volunteer duties include weeding, maintenance, giving tours and organizing fundraising efforts. Volunteer effort goes a long way in maintaining the greenhouse and ensuring that it remains engaged with the community at large.

However, volunteer burnout is a significant challenge in any community-based initiative relying so heavily on sweat equity. The high turnover at the board level and among volunteers is an obstacle the greenhouse confronts on a regular basis, due in large part to the immense amount of work it takes to run such a large project. Another reason behind turnover lies in the transitional nature of the community, to which many people come temporarily or on a seasonal basis. The greenhouse does have a part-time, paid coordinator, but this is a seasonal position and the majority of the work is taken on by the board and community volunteers. A full-time coordinator position would help to alleviate much of the workload stress the greenhouse currently experiences, however, finding funding to support such a position has proved incredibly challenging.

The turnover of board members, staff and volunteers also results in a loss of knowledge, something that affects the relationships the greenhouse shares with is partners. A sustainable long-term vision is required, but in order to create one, strong leadership at the board and community level is necessary, which includes seeking a longer-term commitment from participants.

There are several challenges associated with operating a major greenhouse so far north. The town of Inuvik depends on food and other supplies brought in by plane or up the Dempster Highway, a long stretch of road that travels through Yukon before crossing over the Mackenzie River by ice road or ferry before reaching the town. This significant distance by road and air translates to a much higher cost for goods. Therefore, the soil and bedding plants needed to garden come at a very high price, a challenge that Morrisson and Clarkson aimed to address through the Inuvik Community Greenhouse plan. The greenhouse still has to pay these high costs, however, with the amount of sponsorship it receives, as well as earned revenue through its gift shop, plant sales and fall fair, as well as its ability to buy soil in bulk, the collective costs are more sustainable than what they are for an individual gardener. However, to rely solely on bedding plants and soil brought in from the south is very costly and, with the timing of the river's ice breakup, it is difficult to ensure that supplies arrive in time for the start of the growing season. Therefore, in the second-floor commercial space, the Inuvik Community Garden Society now grows its own bedding plants and hydroponic vegetables, which it sells to local gardeners. This makes the costs associated with garden start-up more economical and keeps more money in the community. Furthermore, the revenue from sales goes directly toward covering the operation and management costs of the greenhouse. Meanwhile, the greenhouse's new composting program also decreases the need to buy compost from the south.

One of the greatest advantages to a greenhouse above the Arctic Circle also poses some additional challenges. With twenty-four-hour sunlight, Inuvik summer days can be excessively hot. A fan was installed to circulate air and help regulate temperature, but even still, delicate greens like lettuce and spinach sometimes perish under the intense heat. By contrast, overcast days can result in wilted produce and fruit like tomatoes rotting on the vine. However, gardeners have adapted to these challenges of Arctic farming by watering regularly and choosing seed varieties carefully. Much of this know-how is shared between gardeners who meet one another in the greenhouse, leading to the development of a new kind of local knowledge in the community.

The Inuvik Community Garden Society continues to receive assistance from territorial, federal and Aboriginal governments, companies in the oil and gas industry and many other businesses. Industry has also been an unlikely source of in-kind support through the donation of time from its plumbers, electricians and other tradespeople to assist with greenhouse maintenance and renovations. In a similar vein, the greenhouse also partners with the Aurora College Trades Access Program. Students have provided carpentry, plumbing and electrical services to the greenhouse. This partnership has been a great resource for ongoing maintenance and also provides a hands-on setting for the training of students.

Another challenge relates to maintaining a sense of community ownership over the greenhouse. With a limited number of plots available, and a long waiting list, greenhouse organizers have to work hard to keep the larger community involved and engaged in greenhouse activities. Community outreach is a key component in the greenhouse's mandate, which is the driver behind the workshops it offers. Through partnerships with other local groups, such as a local quilting guild that displays its quilts in the greenhouse classroom, the community finds many reasons to visit the greenhouse. The gift shop and Saturday market are additional ways in which the wider community is brought into greenhouse activities.

Looking Ahead

The Inuvik Community Greenhouse project is a main focal point in the community. The large, blue building with a curved roof holds within it the bountiful energies of the community and the midnight sun. The project successfully contributes to local food security and at the same time has bolstered the local economy. The Inuvik Community Greenhouse Society hopes to secure funds to allow for a full-time greenhouse coordinator so that more of the society's commercial and community goals can be realized. This is a significant challenge to the organization and its capacity, one that program and greenhouse expansion rests upon. Until then, the greenhouse continues to be an important part of the community's social, economic and physical landscapes and is a significant source of community pride for local residents. Most importantly, it demonstrates the potential for achieving the seemingly impossible when a community unites through innovation, collaboration and a willingness to learn and grow together.

Author's Note

Thank you to Peter Clarkson, as well as to the Inuvik Community Greenhouse, for providing interviews and other background materials for this chapter.

References

Abelson, J., Giacomini, M., Lehoux, P., & Gauvin, F.P. (2007). Bringing "the public" into health technology assessment and coverage policy decisions: From principles to practice. *Health Policy, 82*(1), 37–50.

Chan, H.M., Fediuk, K., Hamilton, S., Rostas, L., Caughey, A., Kuhnlein, H.,... Loring, E. (2006). Food security in Nunavut, Canada: Barriers and recommendations. *International Journal of Circumpolar Health, 65*(5), 416–431.

Dowd, A. (2008). Raising vegetables in Canada's midnight sun. *The Christian Science Monitor.* Retrieved from http://www.csmonitor.com/The-Culture/Gardening/2008/0909/raising-vegetables-in-canadas-midnight-sun

Fillion, M., Laird, B., Douglas, V., Van Pelt, L., Archie, D., & Chan, H.M. (2014). Development of a strategic plan for food security and safety in the Inuvialuit Settlement Region, Canada. *International Journal of Circumpolar Health.* doi:http://dx.doi.org/10.3402%2Fijch.v73.25091

George, J. (2008). The trials and tribulations of home grown vegetables: Ignoring earlier failures, pioneering gardeners vow to bring green revolution to Iqaluit. *Nunatsiaq Online*. Retrieved from http://www.nunatsiaqonline.ca/archives/2008/809/80905/news/features/80905_1499.html

Lambden, J., Receveur, O., Marshall, J., & Kuhnlein, H.V. (2006). Traditional and market food access in Arctic Canada is affected by economic factors. *International Journal of Circumpolar Health, 65*(4), 331–340.

Langston, L. (n.d.). From hockey to horticulture: How a northern community transformed a hockey rink into a greenhouse. *Canadian Gardening Magazine Online*. Retrieved from http://www.canadiangardening.com/gardens/indoor-gardening/from-hockey-to-horticulture/a/1242

Mahoney, J. (2004, July 12). Hothouse flourishes as rink turns over new leaf: Vegetables, flowers—even residents—seem to thrive in Arctic community garden greenhouse. *The Globe and Mail*. Retrieved from http://www.theglobeandmail.com/news/national/hothouse-flourishes-as-rink-turns-over-new-leaf/article4123330/

12

Moses Hernandez
and Rajiv Rawat

The YWCA of Yellowknife

A Turning Point for the Northern Social Economy

The Young Women's Christian Association (YWCA) Yellowknife is one of the most prominent social service organizations in the Canadian North. Its impact in Yellowknife and the Northwest Territories as a whole has been substantial and wide-ranging throughout its fifty-year history. YWCA Yellowknife is also one of the oldest nongovernmental organizations (NGOs) in the Northwest Territories. Since its inception in 1966, the YWCA has grown from a two-staff undertaking to an operation of more than one hundred employees at its peak.

The YWCA offers a range of programs and services, including child and youth programming, shelter and support for women and children fleeing violence, emergency and transitional housing and, up until 2013, the YWCA also provided housing to people with disabilities and mental health issues (for over twenty-seven years and ten years, respectively).

Now entering its sixth decade, YWCA Yellowknife continues to answer the community's call for help by providing an array of services to women, children and families. The YWCA operates numerous programs that help those in poverty or subsisting on low income. These include transitional and emergency housing, life skills counselling and support to help resolve poor tenant issues and to save for damage deposits in the future. The YWCA also operates a twelve-bed shelter for women and children fleeing violence in Yellowknife. In 2014, the YWCA opened Lynn's Place, a brand-new, eighteen-unit, transitional housing building for single women and women with children impacted by domestic violence. Its longstanding commitment to youth has led it to organize programs for children who have witnessed violence and workshops for teens related to dating violence.

The organization has developed organically, evolving and growing based on the needs of individuals, families and government agencies to provide a broad complement of programs and services to Yellowknife's most vulnerable people. Its early objective as part of the international network of YWCAs was to promote the personal development of women. YWCA Yellowknife expanded its mission to, as one of its mottos attests, "increase the well-being and independence of *people*, particularly women" (L. Fuller & J. Green, personal communication, 2012). This expanded mission saw the YWCA addressing the needs of the community for the provision of supportive housing and community inclusion for male and female adults with developmental disabilities and mental health issues. Up until 2013, the YWCA had successfully operated several supportive living group homes and an independent living outreach service for those clients. Indeed, it was the largest provider of housing and housing-related support for both demographic groups in the territory. Therefore, over time, the YWCA broadened its scope toward a more inclusive service delivery in order to fulfill the needs of the community. However, recent changes in the organization's programming have returned YWCA Yellowknife to its original role as a "Turning Point for Women."[1]

History

Throughout much of its history, YWCA Yellowknife has been sustained by a local volunteer board of directors. The local organization, in turn, contributes financially toward the national and international YWCA network. From its modest beginnings in providing housing to single working women, YWCA Yellowknife now manages seven major programs under three separate departments. According to the *2010–2011 YWCA Yellowknife Annual Report*, almost one thousand people accessed at least one of its programs (ranging from the short-term emergency shelter for families to long-term clients of the supported living programs) in that fiscal year.

Housing Support for Employed Young Women

In 1965, Ben Sivertz, the commissioner of the Northwest Territories, invited the YWCA of Canada to establish a small residence for single young women in Yellowknife. He was concerned that there were no affordable accommodations for high school graduates and students, even if there was employment. Helen Law, the first executive director of YWCA Yellowknife, believed that this new YWCA residence would provide women with "help and guidance in adapting to a whole new way of life" (L. Fuller & J. Green, personal communication, 2012). After concerted local fundraising and organizing, the YWCA found itself at 4916 Matonabee Street in a house loaned to it by the government of the Northwest Territories. With the opening of the Matonabee residence, the YWCA was officially inaugurated by Pauline Vanier, wife of Governor General Georges Vanier, on Monday, September 12, 1966. Three years later, YWCA Yellowknife appointed its first local executive director, Ruth Spence, who presided over the organization for its thirteen formative years. The early work of the organization was characterized in *News/North* in 1966 as providing employed young women a home atmosphere in a supervised hostel setting, while gaining work experience, to find wholesome companionship within the northern community, and make the transfer from the school to the social and business community with a minimum of expense.

Adult Recreation and Leisure

In its first twenty years, the YWCA developed sports and recreational programming, including yoga, synchronized swimming, skating, physical fitness, disco and belly dancing. These activities were the organization's public face. However, as the social service role of the YWCA expanded, most of these sport and recreational programs were discontinued, with some later provided by the territorial government and the City of Yellowknife (for example, moms and tots and adult skating programs).

Child Care

In response to strong community need, the YWCA opened the first daycare in the Northwest Territories in January of 1972. In 1974, the first after-school program was initiated at Mildred Hall School. The after-school programs were eventually expanded on a fee-for-service basis to every school in Yellowknife. Because of continuing strong demand, these programs have continued to thrive to this day. However, after establishing several daycare programs throughout the city over the years, YWCA had to end its most recent program in 1998 due to ongoing difficulties with the territorial financial assistance model for daycare. Despite the growing need for quality daycare, the only child care program the YWCA currently delivers is after school.

YWCA Yellowknife also launched Project Child Recovery in 2000, another school-based, national signature YWCA program for children aged six to twelve who have witnessed or been exposed to violence. In the 2013–2014 fiscal year, Project Child Recovery reached out to three hundred children in schools in Yellowknife and N'dilo and the nearby Tłı̨chǫ community of Behchokǫ̀.

More recently, YWCA Yellowknife adopted the national GirlSpace after-school program that serves girls aged eight to seventeen free of charge. The GirlSpace program helps raise awareness of violence and its causes and allows girls to develop positive self-esteem. In the 2009–2010 fiscal year, there were forty-two girls

12.1 Rockhill Residence, 2011.
Courtesy of Rajiv Rawat

enrolled in GirlSpace. In addition to GirlSpace, a new mentoring program for girls aged 11–13 was created in 2014, as well as a year-round resilience training program for boys.

Social Services Programming

In 1978, as a result of the need for more housing accommodation, the YWCA leased eight floors of Northern United Place as office and residential space. The YWCA remained at Northern United Place until 1997, when it was displaced by the new Aurora College campus. That year, the YWCA housing program, known today as the transitional and emergency housing programs for families, moved to the thirty-nine-unit Rockhill apartment complex. In the 2009–2010 fiscal year, Rockhill was home to ninety-nine adults and 127 children. The YWCA experienced financial difficulties in the 1980s due to unsustainable growth, and this period was also marked by a downturn

12.2 Jenifer Rigby, Alison McAteer House shelter manager, speaking with Governor General Adrienne Clarkson during her visit, 2000.
Courtesy of Rajiv Rawat

in the local economy, beginning with the Giant Mine strike in the summer of 1980. Subsequently, the YWCA increasingly tailored the direction of its programming to address the important needs of the city and the territory as a whole, while letting go of programs that could be led by other local organizations. As a result, the YWCA became increasingly involved in social issues. A working group was started to study the need for a crisis centre for women fleeing or experiencing violence. This coincided with the publishing of a self-help booklet for battered women.

As the demand for accommodation and services for victims of spousal assault grew, and as a result of the work of the Transition House Working Group, the government of the Northwest Territories (GNWT) funded the establishment of a transition house at Northern United Place in August 1986. This facility was later named Alison McAteer House, after a former YWCA president and Yellowknife city councillor who passed away suddenly under mysterious circumstances. The Alison McAteer House moved just before the YWCA left Northern United Place to a separate, government-owned, twelve-bed facility. In the 2013–2014 fiscal year, the residence hosted 237 women and children. It remains a fully funded YWCA program through support from both the Yellowknife Health and Social Services Authority (YHSSA) and the GNWT Department of Justice.

Housing and Outreach Support for People with Disabilities

In 1985, the YWCA assumed the management of a group home for eight adults with developmental disabilities. It is important to note that YWCA Yellowknife was one of only two YWCAs in Canada that provided housing services for people with developmental disabilities. Also in 1985, the YWCA took over the management of a group home for senior citizens but closed this residence when the Aven Manor Seniors facility opened in 1987. In April 2003, under contract with the YHSSA, the YWCA began providing support for clients with mental health difficulties living in both group home settings (supported living) and in their own homes (in-home support). That year, the YWCA purchased the first of six homes in Yellowknife for clients, and eventually the group homes and the Independent Living Support (ILS) program became part of YWCA Yellowknife's Department of Community Support Services, which became the largest department of the YWCA, with the largest budget. As a result of this growth, YWCA Yellowknife became the largest provider of housing and support for people with developmental disabilities and mental health conditions in the territory. However, in 2013, a major change occurred when the YHSSA contracts to provide housing and supports to those clients were awarded to other Yellowknife-based nonprofits. While the transition, as could be imagined, was initially challenging for both clients and YWCA staff, this change has allowed the YWCA to concentrate its efforts on other YWCA programs, including new ones.

Financial Trials

With its long history in the Yellowknife community, the YWCA has achieved remarkable success in a number of key areas. Especially important for a nongovernmental organization, the YWCA has established positive, long-standing relations with major funding organizations. In particular, the territorial government and the regional health and social services authority have relied heavily on the YWCA for the delivery of essential social services. In turn, the trust engendered by these long-term relationships has allowed the YWCA to engage on a relatively more equal footing than other agencies with similar financial arrangements.

However, the ongoing dependence on government funding highlights the YWCA's general concern about its increasingly contingent nature. This vulnerability is felt more at the time of contract renewal, when programs can come to an abrupt end due to any type of shift in government policy. Moreover, this unequal relationship inevitably, if inadvertently, leads to pervasive government control over organizational decision making. By funding programs the government selects rather than what the YWCA or similar organizations believe are important, priorities are subordinated to government mandates and nongovernmental autonomy is curtailed. In the worst instance, such organizations run the risk of being reduced to poorly funded adjuncts of the YHSSA.

This loss of control has also been felt in collaborative ventures with the City of Yellowknife and the Northwest Territories Housing Corporation. Despite twenty-five years in the housing field, municipal and territorial agencies have often dismissed the YWCA's proposals on floor plans and sustainable designs that have been based on its own learned experiences. In controlling the purse strings, cost-cutting priorities have otherwise dominated, giving rise to entirely foreseeable problems cropping up in the future.

In Yellowknife, in particular, these financial constraints have been compounded by the challenge of attracting and retaining skilled employees. As a nonprofit with a lower rate of pay for commensurate work, staff turnover is a chronic problem for

YWCA's front-line services. Although the YWCA has established good working relationships with the YHSSA, this essential service delivery depends on the YWCA's ability to hire and retain staff in a very competitive job market. Ensuring that NGO salaries remain comparable to government employees who do similar work is one way of addressing the challenge, but the wage gap remains almost insurmountably large. This discrepancy is even starker for casual employees who also go without benefits. Nevertheless, the YWCA has been able to secure long-term funding for select services, such as Alison McAteer House, and financial stability has also been a major, if rare, achievement for a nonprofit in recent lean times. Moreover, the YWCA has, on occasion, pared back or eliminated programs that were no longer financially viable. This was the principal reason for the YWCA withdrawing completely from the daycare sector in 1998, despite the fact that such services were desperately needed in a market where choices have remained limited and expensive. When the YWCA did offer the service, it was well received, but the organization could not continue to support it. Unfortunately, for low-income earners, existing options remain an overwhelming burden. The YWCA continues to receive requests to relaunch the service.

Donations have been strategically invested in areas such as home renovation, so that expenses can be reduced in the long run. At the Rockhill transitional housing complex, the GNWT and the diamond corporation De Beers funded the installation of water-saving devices such as low-flow shower heads and taps, low-flush toilets and front-loading washing machines. From 2010 to 2011, these measures reduced water bills by 13 per cent, a not insignificant savings given the high cost of utilities for such buildings in the North. Programmable thermostats and hallway temperature set-backs also helped save eleven thousand litres of heating oil. This has been especially important given that such residential programs often run at a loss. In Rockhill, only a few spaces are funded through the GNWT, while rent, fundraising and even earnings from coin-operated laundry machines sustain the rest.

Extending the Reach

As demonstrated by its extensive role in housing people with developmental disabilities, as well as providing services to male clients, YWCA Yellowknife has developed in several distinct policy directions that have made it unique among the national network of local YWCA chapters. It has striven to fill specific social needs in a northern context and has evolved and adapted along with the community's changing demographics.

An important goal has been to extend the "Y's" reach beyond Yellowknife. The capital city has remained a major destination for young women looking for work, seeking education or escaping troubles in their communities. However, the YWCA has continued to look for ways to extend its program footprint throughout the North, where the needs are also great. For instance, YWCA Yellowknife recently commenced operation of the Sutherland House family violence shelter in Fort Smith, as it did from 2005 to 2008 in response to a request from the regional health and social services authority following the collapse of the society that ran the shelter up until that point.

YWCA Yellowknife has also provided chapter-to-chapter support, stepping into the breach to help prevent the closure of Iqaluit's family violence shelter in 2007. Operated by the Baffin Region Agvvik Society, Qimaavik Women's Shelter was able to remain open due to Yellowknife's efforts to procure funds from the national YWCA. This was followed by YWCA Canada opening Sivummut House, a homeless women's shelter, in 2009. Both shelters are, in turn, operated by YWCA Agvvik Nunavut, which emerged from the merger of the Agvvik Society and the YWCA.

The YWCA likewise identified staffing capacity for shelters as a major need and accordingly developed training modules for prospective staff across the North. Such training not only ensured that facilities meet the standards of government funders but also "added value" to northern communities by enabling local people to provide a greater level of care.

Research and Advocacy

The YWCA also procured funding and served as one of the lead organizations for both a NWT-focused and pan-territorial research program on women and homelessness. These culminated in two published reports in 2007 titled, *You Just Blink and It Can Happen: A Study of Women's Homelessness North of 60°*, and *Being Homeless Is Getting to Be Normal: A Study of Women's Homelessness in the Northwest Territories*. The research projects brought together a wide network of women's organizations across the three territories to map the determinants, impacts and service environment in which women's homelessness is addressed, as well as to inform public policy and advocate for community action. Researchers documented the voices of the homeless, as well as those of service providers, while reviewing the field of practice from both nonprofit and governmental perspectives. In addition to highlighting oral testimony and appraising the existing system of care, the comprehensive final report listed a series of detailed proposals for improving the situation in the North.

In 2010, the YWCA worked in conjunction with the Yellowknife-based social justice group Alternatives North and a number of other social service organizations to organize a two-day No Place for Poverty—Anti-Poverty Workshop that attracted eighty delegates from twenty communities in the Northwest Territories. In concert with the No Place for Poverty campaign to prompt multisector development of a territorial anti-poverty strategy, the workshop picked up where the homelessness study left off and brought together the principal social sector organizations in the territory in order to begin a conversation that would lead to direct policy recommendations for the GNWT. Similar efforts across the country led to the successful adoption of anti-poverty or poverty-reduction strategies in a majority of the provinces, as well as commitments from Yukon and Nunavut to proceed further. Through the concerted efforts of organizations such as the YWCA and Alternatives North, eighteen out of nineteen MLAs pledged (during the 2011 territorial elections) to work on an anti-poverty strategy as a priority in the seventeenth legislative assembly.

While the hard work continues toward the reduction and elimination of poverty in the territory from all levels of government and sectors, there has been significant progress toward achieving that objective, including the release of the GNWT Anti-Poverty Strategic Framework (2013) and the Anti-Poverty Roundtable discussions (in 2013 and 2014) that will help guide a multistakeholder action plan. The YWCA continues to play an active and prominent role in contributing input toward the action plan. The participation of the YWCA is a key element in the multistakeholder process and this is due to the organization's long history and experience of providing essential programs and services to a diverse range of low-income and disadvantaged individuals and families over several decades in Yellowknife, in particular, and the territory, in general.

In addition to the various advocacy and research initiatives mentioned earlier, the YWCA has been a key member of the Yellowknife Homelessness Coalition, a multisector and multistakeholder alliance that formed to find collaborative solutions to the emerging homelessness challenges in Yellowknife. In addition to compiling a homeless report card in 2008 and engaging in significant social and statistical analysis of local homelessness issues, the coalition's efforts resulted in the creation of Bailey House, a transitional housing complex for men completed in 2009 and operated by the Salvation Army. In 2014, the coalition morphed into the Community Advisory Board (CAB) on homelessness to oversee the development of community plans—a requirement in order to access capital funding under the Federal Homelessness Partnering Strategy. The YWCA's experience and knowledge of providing various supported and supportive housing options for people with mental illness has also been an important resource for CAB's current focus on the implementation of homelessness projects in Yellowknife based on a Housing First model.

With the support of the coalition, the YWCA, after many years of dedication, as well as challenges, realized its vision of providing women transitional housing as a "Better Environment to Transition in Yellowknife" in the creation of Betty House (L. Fuller & J. Green, personal communication, 2012). The YWCA was selected to be the operator of the Betty House early on in the planning process and was so deeply vested in the project/vision since that time that the organization provided its own financial contributions to the construction of the building (the majority of the funding was provided through a combination of federal funding and private-sector contributions). Following the Betty House opening ceremony on September 26, 2014, it was renamed the Lynn Brooks' Safe Place for Women (commonly referred to as "Lynn's Place"). Lynn's Place is alternatively called *Hoti Etsanda Ko*, meaning "healthy living place" in the Weledeh dialect of the Tłįchǫ language. The building itself is made up of eighteen units on three floors. There are six units for single women, ten two-bedroom units and two three-bedroom units. As a transitional housing complex for women and children whose lives have been impacted by domestic violence, it is the first of its kind in Yellowknife. Lynn's Place opened its doors to new occupants in October 2014.

Conclusion

With its solid record of growth and achievement, YWCA Yellowknife has established itself as a unique and important chapter of the global women's federation. It has conformed remarkably to the social realities of the North, dispensing with traditional YWCA activities better supported by other organizations and evolving to fit the needs of the community. Moreover, this has enabled the YWCA to leverage its strength to help other social economy organizations while extending its reach throughout the North.

While the YWCA has transitioned out of delivering housing programs and support to some client groups, it is repositioned to be a leader in other areas with high needs and demand, particularly in the delivery of transitional housing for women. It has established a solid record of financial management, operating a $5-million budget in 2010–2011 with a small surplus.

As seen with its important role in the Yellowknife Homelessness Coalition or No Place for Poverty campaign, the YWCA has also continued to participate in important initiatives while playing a central role in the social fabric of the city. That the YWCA can fulfill such diverse mandates demonstrates the social economy ideal of fulfilling basic human needs while attending to a longer-term vision of a society based on equality, social inclusion and dignity.

Authors' Note

We would like to thank the following staff members of YWCA Yellowknife for agreeing to be interviewed for this chapter: Lyda Fuller, Julie Green, Dianne Jamieson and Janette Morris.

Note

1. This is the current national motto of the YWCA. YWCA Yellowknife continues to provide programming for children and youth, including empowerment programs for girls and boys (L. Fuller & J. Green, personal communication, 2012).

References

Alternatives North & YWCA Yellowknife. (2010, October). *No place for poverty—Anti-poverty workshop report*. Retrieved from http://aged.alternativesnorth.ca/pdf/NoPlaceForPovertyReport_email.pdf

Bopp, J. (2007a). *You just blink and it can happen: A study of women's homelessness north of 60*. Cochrane, AB: Four Worlds Development Centre.

Bopp, J. (2007b). *Being homeless is getting to be normal: A study of women's homelessness in the Northwest Territories*. Cochrane, AB: Four Worlds Development Centre.

Carmichael, D. (2014, September 29). Yellowknife transitional home opens with new name. *Northern Journal*. Retrieved from http://norj.ca/2014/09/yellowknife-transitional-home-opens-with-new-name/

Falvo, N. (2011). *Homelessness in Yellowknife: An emerging social challenge*. Toronto, ON: The Canadian Homelessness Research Network Press.

Government of the Northwest Territories. (2014). *Sharing, love and respect: Report on the deliberations of the 2014 NWT anti-poverty round table*. Retrieved from http://www.assembly.gov.nt.ca/sites/default/files/td201-175.pdf

News/North, November 3, 1966, n.p.

Yellowknife Homeless Coalition. (2007). *Planning for phase III of the community plan to address homelessness in Yellowknife*. Yellowknife, NT: Author.

YWCA Yellowknife. (1986). Our past...our future. Yellowknife, NT: Author.

YWCA Yellowknife. (2011). *Annual report 2010–2011*. Retrieved from http://www.ywcanwt.ca/documents/YWCA%20AnReport%202011%20OnLine.pdf

YWCA Yellowknife. (2014). *Annual report 2013–2014*. Retrieved from http://www.ywcanwt.ca/about-ywca/annual-report

13

Kiri Staples

Yukon Artists @ Work Co-operative

Co-operatives have been used as a business model for community development across Canada (Gibson, 2005), with some particularly prominent co-operatives located within the country's northern regions. On an international scale, co-operatives (co-ops) are being recognized for the potential role they can play in the development of rural and marginalized communities (Hardy, 2009). This role is exemplified by the growth of organizations such as Arctic Co-operatives Ltd. in the Northwest Territories and Nunavut. Yukon, however, is an exception to these trends with only a handful of co-operatives managing to keep their doors open. One of the few success stories in the territory is the Yukon Artists @ Work Co-operative (YAAW), a group of dedicated local artists that independently run an art gallery in Whitehorse, Yukon.

An affinity between co-operatives and the arts sector has long been established. In the North, the first co-operatives were formed in the 1960s to market traditional Aboriginal arts and crafts (Hardy, 2009). By the 1980s, the co-operative business model had grown rapidly, expanding into fishing, retail, community banking and hotels (Ironside, 2000). Today, it is acknowledged that Aboriginal co-operatives in the Arctic make significant economic contributions to the communities they are located in (Ketilson & MacPherson, 2001). Artist co-operatives are still an important part of this sector. For example, Alsop and MacPherson (2010) explore the substantial role that the West Baffin/Kinngait Co-operative has played in Cape Dorset, a community that is said to have more artists per capita than any other community in Canada. Similar stories can be found across the Arctic (e.g., Berlo, 1989; Graburn, 2000; Ketilson & MacPherson, 2001).

The artists that make up these co-ops work together as an organization to provide space and infrastructure to work on, exhibit and sell their art. Members share financial and work responsibilities, as well as costs for the rent, utilities and maintenance of their site. This arrangement has in many cases been a recipe for success for various types and groups of artists. The Yukon Artists @ Work Co-operative is one such organization. The real strength of YAAW, though, does not lie in its organizational structure. Rather, it is its connection to the people and organizations of Yukon and the support network it offers the arts community that is the foundation for the co-operative's success. On one side of this relationship, encouragement from community members has taken various forms, ranging from bringing visitors in to the art gallery or lobbying on behalf of the co-operative. Nonprofit organizations and businesses alike have been equally as supportive, offering creative and innovative partnerships for the benefit of both parties. Another aspect of this relationship is the way in which YAAW has brought individual artists from across the territory together, offering not only a space to sell their work but a sense of community. In this way, the Yukon Artists @ Work Co-operative offers a unique narrative of a social economy organization that has forged its own success, at times against significant odds.

History

In August of 2002, three artists came together with the purpose of starting a society to support local artists in Yukon. Although previous attempts had been made to create such a group, these attempts had not come to fruition. In the past, there was always an element missing, such as timing or the right fit of people. This time around, all the elements seemed to be in place. By the end of August, the group's numbers doubled to six members. As awareness of their activities spread, this growth continued and by September they grew to nine. In October of that year, a total of twelve artists organized themselves into a society called the Yukon Artists @ Work (later known as the Yukon Artists @ Work Co-operative). In a small trailer near the outskirts of Whitehorse's city limits, the group set up its first art gallery. The opening was an incredible success. Not only was there an impressive turnout of community members to the event but the artists sold around $12,000 worth of their work.

Six weeks later, members of YAAW were given the opportunity to expand out of their small but successful trailer gallery. The group's landlord owned a large, metal, industrial building in the same neighbourhood that she offered to convert into a new gallery. Although several of the artists thought this upgrade would be too expensive for such a fledgling organization, the group had no problem finding more local artists to become members and contribute to the move. Thus, by March 2003, Yukon Artists @ Work was able to open a new, larger gallery, filled with pieces from over thirty Yukon artists. Once again, the opening night for the gallery was an unprecedented event, with cars lined up along the Alaska Highway waiting to see what the group had created. Previous sales records were also surpassed, with over $20,000 of art sales being made over the course of the day.

The sheer volume of support that the YAAW gallery received in these initial months was demonstrative of the gap that existed in the arts sector and the ongoing need for a venue of this sort. Previously, there were very few options for professional-level artists looking for a commercial gallery space in the territory. Moreover, many of the spaces that did advertise themselves as galleries primarily operated

as gift shops, as this is the only way to survive in a high-rent district such as downtown Whitehorse. The newly established Yukon Artists @ Work gallery, however, was able to set itself apart by operating as the only artist-run gallery in the territory that sold solely original, Yukon-made work. The sacrifice, however, was that it operated in a low-rent area outside the central hub of downtown business.
In 2010, the YAAW artists were able to improve the strategic location of their gallery, though this decision to move was not one that was undertaken willingly. After six years at their location in the McCrae subdivision, the artists were evicted when unstable economic conditions meant the building's landlord had to seek more economically viable tenants (Belik, 2010). They were given one month to find a new space for their gallery. Fortunately, the group was able to capitalize on the circumstances at hand and found a new location closer to the city centre but still on the outskirts of the downtown core. Although the new building was smaller and the rent more expensive, the gallery benefitted from an increased number of visitors. The members who operate Yukon Artists @ Work also had to adapt to this location in other ways. For the first time, their doors were open on weekdays for the entire year. Previously, the gallery was open for seven days a week in the summer and only on weekends in the winter. With the new location's higher rent, they now kept their doors open for several days during the week during the winter months. Building on this momentum, they recently decided to move their location yet again to a central downtown location. In order to raise the funds required for such a move, they started a crowdfunding campaign, which once again far surpassed their expectations.

The time and effort that has been put into the gallery is evident. The gallery is home to an eclectic yet complementary collection of different art forms, from colourful felted scarves to intricately engraved knives, photographs to paintings, carvings to furniture. The result is a gallery that showcases the best that Yukon artists have to offer. For Harreson Tanner, a founding member of Yukon Artists @ Work and the gallery manager, it is no surprise that things have come together so well: "When you get 25 to 30 creative artists

13.1 The new Yukon Artists @ Work gallery located in downtown Whitehorse, 2015.
Courtesy of Valoree Walker

together you'll always get an interesting space in the end" (Belik, 2010). Locals and visitors alike have recognized the exhibited talent. In 2005, Travelocity.ca chose the Yukon Artists @ Work gallery as one of North America's top picks for its "Local Secrets, Big Finds" campaign. In 2007, the gallery was visited by then Governor General Michaëlle Jean. This trend has continued, with government offices frequently bringing out-of-town guests from across Canada and around the world for private tours.

Structure and Operations

One of the defining features of the co-operative is that it is entirely run by its membership, which is open only to Yukon artists. There are currently thirty-five members, nine of whom are from rural communities in the territory. This number has changed periodically over time. At one point, when still at their McCrae location, YAAW reached a high of forty-four members. Conversely, the organization has also experienced tougher times. When the artists were evicted from the McCrae gallery, they had only twenty-four members. This lack of resources made their move to a new location all the more difficult.

Membership with YAAW is targeted mainly toward established artists rather than emerging ones. When requests for membership are submitted, a committee reviews the application. The decision to either grant or deny membership is then based on artistic merit, education (formal, self-taught or a combination of both), experience exhibiting and overall quality of work. Once accepted, members pay a one-time, nonrefundable fee of $100 to join Yukon Artists @ Work, as well as a regular contribution of a dollar a day (or $30 a month) that goes toward the upkeep of the gallery. In addition, the organization takes a 25 per cent commission cut from what is sold and members must work a number of shifts at the gallery over the course of the year. For artists who live outside Whitehorse, another level of membership is available, which takes a 35 per cent commission but allows them exemption from working regular shifts at the gallery. Instead, these out-of-town members must come in once a year and provide a demonstration of their art form. In addition to running the gallery, several of the co-operative's members are also on the board of directors that governs the organization. There are currently seven members on the board, which is open only to members of YAAW. As a result of this structure, those involved in Yukon Artists @ Work represent a variety of artists who are deeply invested in an organization that they both own and operate. Moreover, these feelings are apparent in the atmosphere of the gallery itself. Visitors are able to meet with the artists as they walk through the gallery, creating a welcoming and interactive environment.

Yukon Artists @ Work is further able to set itself apart because of its distinctive role as one of the territory's few successful co-operatives. A co-operative is defined as "any enterprise that is collectively owned and democratically controlled by its members for their mutual benefit" (Hardy, 2009). These organizations contribute significantly to the Canadian economy. With over nine thousand co-ops in the country, they have almost eighteen million members (along with credit unions), employ over 150,000 people and control assets totalling over $330 billion (Canadian Co-operative Association, n.d.). Moreover, in northern Canada co-operatives tend to be more successful and larger in terms of volume of business, number of employees and amount of assets than their counterparts in the south (Hardy, 2009). Arctic Co-operatives Ltd., which has steadily grown since the 1950s to boast revenues of $95.4 million, is perhaps the best example of just how successful co-ops in the North can be (Hardy, 2009).

In 2009, a research project undertaken by Lionais and Hardy looked at the factors behind the relative lack of co-op development in Yukon compared to the rest of northern Canada. It found that at the time of the project, there were only four operating co-operatives in the territory. Yet across the northern territories there were a total of fifty-two co-ops (Hardy, 2009). The researchers identified four key areas that have typically contributed to the success of a co-op. These included government support and awareness of co-ops, co-op advocacy and leadership, financing and access to capital and demographic attitudes and economic environment. In Yukon, they found these aspects to be decidedly lacking (Hardy, 2009).

Despite this environment, in which little support is in place for co-operative development, Yukon Artists @ Work manages to operate as a co-operative. However, the organization did not initially structure itself according to this model. When YAAW first opened, it was run as a nonprofit society. This changed in 2006, when a local merchant took issue with the fact that it had nonprofit status yet appeared to sell art for a profit. Artist Harreson Tanner counters this argument by pointing out that in the case of Yukon Artists @ Work, there is a difference between the organization and the artists themselves. He explains that YAAW exists to provide an organizing body, infrastructure and space for artists to sell their work. When a piece is sold, it is the artist who receives the payment. The 25–35 per cent commission that the organization receives from this sale is put toward the operation of the gallery and maintenance of the facility. Most years, this revenue has barely been enough to keep the doors open.

In effect, Yukon Artists @ Work initially operated as a non-profit group. Yet the fact that YAAW does not make a profit as an organization failed to be understood. As a result, the group was forced by the government to dissolve and reform as a co-operative. This change was primarily a formality as the organization continues to operate in a similar way as before. As a co-operative, it is governed by the users of its services (its members). Unlike some co-operatives, though, there is no dispensing of extra funds to shareholders at the end of the year. In the rare case that there are excess funds, they are invested back into the organization. Consequently, YAAW exists as a nonprofit co-operative, rather than simply one or the other.

Successes, Collaborations and Challenges

The advantages of running an artist co-operative include shared costs, networking and educational opportunities, while the disadvantages highlighted are the high workloads, fee requirements and shared agreements and decisions. For YAAW members, the designation of co-op has also had both positive and negative effects. On the one hand, the co-op model has contributed to the success of the gallery. Bob Atkinson, one of the Yukon Artists @ Work members, points out that there have been a number of art galleries in Yukon that have had to close their doors after only a year or two of operating. He argues that the difference between these galleries and the co-operative gallery lies in the fact that the others are businesses, run with the purpose of making a profit. In contrast, "we are just happy to keep the doors open" (B. Atkinson, personal communication, July 2011). Lise Merchant, another YAAW member, observes that it has also influenced public perception of the organization: "The public has been very supportive, I think because we are a co-operative" (personal communication, July 2011). For individual artists, there is also the added advantage of receiving a better percentage of the profits of their work in comparison to other non-co-operative galleries.

In other ways, the co-operative model has been a barrier for Yukon Artists @ Work. The organization is economically independent yet is desperately in need of funding for administrative and core staff. Currently, Tanner works the majority of the shifts at the gallery, a situation that allows the organization to stay in a viable position but is by no means sustainable. And, yet, there is very little funding available for co-operatives in the territory. This gap is highlighted by Hardy (2009), who further identifies the need for co-op-targeted investment by the government, corporations and other stakeholders in Yukon.

Consequently, Yukon Artists @ Work has found itself in the predicament of being forced by the government to operate as a co-operative but has no support from it for pursuing this model. To compound this, its position as a co-operative has meant that YAAW is unable to access the significant financial support for the arts that exists in the territory. The Yukon government offers a number of programs, such as the Cultural Industry Training Fund, the Arts Fund and the Arts Operating Fund, that are targeted toward the local arts community. However, because it is defined as a co-operative and not a registered nonprofit society, YAAW is not eligible for many of these programs.

The failure of the territorial government to support co-operatives in the region has continued despite the international recognition that co-operatives have gained for their contribution to socio-economic development. This recognition culminated in the designation of 2012 as the International Year of the Co-operative by the United Nations General Assembly, with the slogan "Co-operative Enterprises Build a Better World." In doing so, the UN encouraged its members to promote co-operatives and raise awareness of their potential contribution toward achieving social and economic development objectives, such as the Millennium Development Goals. The International Year of Co-operatives encouraged governments to create national mechanisms, such as national committees, policies and laws that facilitate the creation, growth and sustainability of co-operatives (United Nations, n.d.; Yukon Artists @ Work, n.d.). This initiative points to the need for broader supports for co-operatives worldwide.

13.2 Inside the Yukon Artists @ Work Gallery, 2016.
Courtesy of Valoree Walker

The challenges that Yukon Artists @ Work face must be placed in the broader context of the arts sector in the North. In this setting, artists in Yukon are fortunate to have a significant support system. The Yukon Cultural Industries Labour Force study from 2004 found that over 735 Yukoners earn their living in cultural occupations, with the number of artists or creative workers doubling in the last decade. It is evident that there is a large amount of creative talent in Yukon (Zanasi, Taggart, & Leaf, 2004). The arts community in a city such as Yellowknife, Tanner explains, may be just as vibrant as Whitehorse's, but its capacity to display and sell its work is not even close to what is available in Yukon. He points out that the territory has more cultural facilities per capita than anywhere else in Canada. Despite this, those in Yukon employed in artistic occupations earn less than half the average Yukon income (Zanasi et al., 2004). With the cost of living on the rise, this has meant that artists have had to take three or four part-time jobs in order to support their artwork. Furthermore, the ups and downs of the economy have a significant influence on the arts; when times are hard, many people put the arts on the back burner. During these periods, Tanner explains that those at YAAW try to encourage people to understand that "the art in a community is the soul of a community, if you cut that part of your life out, you become soulless" (personal communication, July 2011).

The relationship between the Yukon Artists @ Work Co-operative and the arts community, as well as with other community members, has been central to the operation of the organization since it opened its doors in 2002. The support from those in Whitehorse and the surrounding areas has consistently demonstrated the way in which the community takes ownership over the co-op. Opening events bring in a crowd larger than many events Tanner has seen outside Yukon. On a daily basis, 60–65 per cent of the business the gallery receives is from local residents (H. Tanner, personal communication, July 2011). According to artist Lise Merchant, "the public has been incredible in terms of support—they're the ones that keep you running" (personal communication, July 2011). The positive feedback from the community is housed in the guest books the gallery keeps. For Tanner, this encouragement is often what keeps him going when the organization faces hard times, because "when it's all volunteer driven, you sometimes need to hear those things just to wake up in the morning" (personal communication, July 2011).

The local business community has played a similarly important role as a champion for Yukon Artists @ Work. This was especially important when the co-op was looking for a new location and found a number of advocates for its cause among the businesses in downtown Whitehorse. Business owners have also done well to recognize the importance of having such a venue for Yukon artists by pursuing collaborations with YAAW. One such partnership is called the Culture Cruiser, a relatively recent undertaking of Yukon Artists @ Work. Although the project was slow to start due to a lack of administrative staff and a driver, the concept is a promising one. The "cruiser," a twelve-passenger van, takes visitors to five locations around Whitehorse that showcase Yukon's distinct cultural environment. Included in the tour are the YAAW gallery, the Yukon Arts Centre, the Yukon Beringia Interpretive Centre, the Yukon Transportation Museum and the MacBride Museum of Yukon History. With the Culture Cruiser as a base, YAAW has sought to expand this project to incorporate partnerships with other downtown businesses. A new Culture Feast project currently being developed proposes working with two local restaurants. After a special lunch, the cruiser would pick up visitors, take them for a private gallery tour and then return them to their hotel. A similar deal is being sought with Yukon Brewery.

Tanner admits that collaboration has not been as consistent as it could have been in the past but hopes that this will change in the future. Yukon Artists @ Work has the ability to offer a distinct Yukon cultural experience, which it aims to integrate into established tourist activities. In the future, it hopes to work with Air North in developing a ground tour operation by offering the Culture Cruiser services as well as artist workshops. It also aims to add a cultural component to the program of a high-end winter tour group. In both cases, the relationship is meant to be mutually beneficial; YAAW will receive more visitors for its part, and tourism operators will be able to offer a more diverse package.

One of the organization's greatest successes, according to Tanner, is the support network that the co-operative has established within the arts community. This system has allowed its members to gain exposure to other artists and opportunities outside Yukon. For artist Bob Atkinson, it gives Yukon artists "a place of their own" (personal communication, July 2011). Most importantly, it has brought together individuals who previously worked in isolation. When going through tough times, artists now have a group of people they know and trust to call upon. For Tanner, this concept is "worth its weight in gold" (personal communication, July 2011).

The strength of this network stems in part from the organization's dedication to social responsibility, which has been explicitly written into its mandate. Not only has YAAW worked with other nonprofit groups such as Blood Ties Four Directions but it has also hosted numerous fundraisers for artists and their families when they are injured. One initiative the organization undertook was to create an artist relief fund. After fundraising over $10,000 in May 2011, it was able to establish a separate society, the Artist Relief Fund Society, dedicated to helping injured artists. This ability of the arts community to respond so quickly and so decisively to a crisis further strengthens its support network and helps people to know and care for one another. And, according to Tanner, "that's part of living in the North" (personal communication, July 2011). Moreover, this support system extends further to influence those who visit the gallery. Tanner explains, "When you're feeling blue, to go into the gallery and meet someone who has the courage to stand on the edge of the cliff every day and create from their very soul, and hope that somebody likes it and buys it, and that's how they live, it gives you the sense that everything will be OK" (personal communication, July 2011).

These accomplishments have not only been appreciated by those within the territory's arts community but also by those beyond Yukon's borders. The group has been approached by others from as far away as Siberia looking to develop a similar organization, using the Yukon Artists @ Work Co-operative as a blueprint. In regards to this sort of collaboration, Tanner acknowledges that the co-op has certainly done a lot of things right and that there are lessons to be learned from its experiences. Nonetheless, he admits there is also a lot that it needs to do better, a promising statement for how the organization will develop in the future.

The Yukon Artists @ Work Co-operative plays a distinct role in the social economy of Yukon. As one of the territory's few successful co-operatives, it has set an example for others pursuing this channel of community development in the North. However, this position has also meant that it faces significant challenges in its work. Due to the lack of government support for co-operatives in the region, YAAW has fallen through the cracks when looking for funding to sustain and expand its operations. Nonetheless, the group continues to thrive because of its relationship with the broader arts community and the support it receives from Yukon community members, organizations and businesses. Central to understanding the story of YAAW's success is the fact that it has managed to create an avenue of cultural tourism that benefits the community, visitors and artists alike. It is this ability that makes the organization a model to consider in the face of a rapidly changing socio-economic environment.

Author's Note

I would like to thank the following members of the Yukon Artists @ Work Co-operative for providing information for this chapter: Harreson Tanner, Bob Atkinson and Lise Merchant.

References

Alsop, J., & MacPherson, I. (2010). *History of Cape Dorset and the West Baffin Co-operative* (Working paper, draft, University of Victoria). Retrieved from http://www.learningcentre.coop/resource/history-cape-dorset-and-west-baffin-co-operative

Belik, V. (2010, April, 7). Yukon artists homeless. *The Yukon News*. Retrieved from http://www.yukon-news.com/news/17510/

Berlo, J. (1989). Inuit women and graphic arts: Female creativity and its cultural context. *The Canadian Journal of Native Studies, 2*, 293–315.

Canadian Co-operative Association. (n.d.). The power of co-operation: Co-operatives and credit unions in Canada. Retrieved from http://www.coopscanada.coop/assets/firefly/files/files/CCAbrochure-English2.pdf

Gibson, R. (2005). *The role of cooperatives in community economic development* (RDI Working Paper #2005-3). Brandon, MB: Rural Development Institute, Brandon University.

Graburn, N. (2000). Canadian Inuit art and coops: Father Steinmann of Povungnituk. *Museum Anthropology, 24*(1), 14–25.

Hardy, K. (2009, March). *Yukon coops final report for MBA (CED), Cape Breton University*. Retrieved from http://yukonresearch.yukoncollege.yk.ca/frontier/files/sernnoca/YukonCoopsMREFinal.pdf

Ironside, R.G. (2000, August). Canadian northern settlements: Top-down and bottom-up influences. *Geografiska Annaler: Series B, Human Geography, 82*(2), 103–114.

Ketilson, L.H., & Macpherson, I. (2001). *A report on Aboriginal co-operatives in Canada: Current situation and potential for growth*. Saskatoon, SK: Centre for the Study of Co-operatives, University of Saskatchewan.

Lionais, D., & Hardy, K. (2009). *Co-operation in the North: Understanding co-operatives in the Yukon* (Final report for the Social Economy Research Network of Northern Canada). Retrieved from http://yukonresearch.yukoncollege.yk.ca/frontier/files/sernnoca/YukonCoopsFinalReportShort.pdf

United Nations. (n.d.). International year of co-operatives 2012. Retrieved from http://social.un.org/coopsyear/index.html

Zanasi, L., Taggart, M., & Leaf, W. (2004, February). *Yukon cultural industries labour force study*. Retrieved from http://www.yukonomics.ca/reports/Yukon_Cultural_Labour_Force.pdf

14

Valoree Walker,
Joseph Moise
and Kiri Staples

Raven Recycling

Raven Recycling, based in Whitehorse, is one of the few social enterprises that operates in Yukon and has a long-standing track record of success. It did not always recognize that its mode of operation put it into this group of social economy organizations. A social enterprise is defined as a business whose products, revenue, purchasing and/or employment practices directly support social, cultural and/or environmental goals, and whose surpluses are reinvested for that purpose (Demonstrating Value, 2009). Social enterprises empower community members to address needs and create change (Vink, 2010). Raven Recycling has not only created a facility but also established a culture of recycling in Yukon. Its programs and mode of operation demonstrate commitment to having recycling as a priority for Yukon waste management strategies.

The case study presented in this chapter highlights the history and operations of Raven Recycling and the significant role that this social enterprise plays in successfully addressing areas of waste management. Starting from just a few concerned citizens,

Raven Recycling has evolved into a Yukon enterprise that had total revenues of $2,834,113 in 2010 (CharityFocus Imagine Canada, n.d.). As a nonprofit society, Raven subsidizes Yukon recycling. It is willing to handle the vast majority of Whitehorse's recycling at a financial loss. As Munson (2010) states, "This is a business that works with a conscience to recycle the Yukon's non-refundable waste using the profits from refundable recyclables." These nonrefundable materials include cardboard, paper, plastics, Styrofoam, milk cartons, Tetra Paks and tin. It is its social aims that dominate the goals of this organization. As with other nonprofit recycling organizations, Raven must work closely with other groups to achieve its intended goals. Support and program development occurs in cooperation with the Whitehorse municipality and Yukon government to ensure that operations can continue and grow.

As our society becomes more acutely aware of human impacts on the environment, the goal of reducing the amount of waste that ends up in our landfills is becoming increasingly important. Collectively, we are beginning to realize that consumer lifestyles simply produce too much waste to be sustainable for much longer. Globally, high priority is often given to recycling programs as part of waste management strategies (Tremblay, Tuberlet, & Peredo, 2010). Progress has been made in the social economy sector, where community and the environment take precedence over profit and traditional values of "economic growth." Recycling organizations across Canada that use nonprofit, socially oriented business models are proving to be leaders in this area. They take a firm stand for achieving sustainable waste objectives with targets aimed at a "zero waste" society (Raven Recycling, n.d.-c). The Raven Recycling Society is one of these organizations. It is often featured regularly in the local media and has a high level of local support. During the twenty-three years of its operation, Raven has grown steadily, expanded its services, weathered the storm of the 2008 global financial crisis and continued to have a significant and positive impact on Yukon. Recycling is a part of everyday life for Yukon people today (Rifkind, 2009a).

14.1 Entrance of the main sorting area for the refundable materials at Raven Recycling, 2014.
Courtesy of Valoree Walker

History

When Raven Recycling was founded in 1989, it operated as the Recycling Committee of the Yukon Conservation Society (YCS). Members of YCS who wanted to see a recycling program started in Yukon began volunteering their time at the Pop Can Depot, which was the only service offered by the committee at the time. Not only was it run exclusively by this group of dedicated volunteers but the initial, single-penny refund for a pop can came directly from the volunteers' pockets. The operations moved from the Jim Light Arena to the Rinkbinder Building, where, in 1990, a part-time manager was hired (Graham & Associates Management Consultants, 1993). In 1992, the Yukon government launched the Beverage/Container Recycling Program, which, at the time, was well ahead of other provincial and territorial recycling initiatives. Along with increasing the bottle depot customers' refund from one to ten cents per can, the initiative also got those at Raven Recycling thinking "that if people were given the incentive to bring back refundables, they would also start to bring their recyclables" (Snyder & McInroy, 2011). Initially, this proved to be true, as there was an emphasis on membership back then that does not exist today. In recent years, however, Raven employees have noticed two different types of clients: refunders and recyclers. Despite its humble beginnings, the recycling committee had grand ambitions for the future of recycling in Yukon. Raven's goal was to reduce the waste stream entering Yukon landfills by 50 per cent by the year 2000 (Graham & Associates Management Consultants, 1993). Its mission then, as it remains today, is "to divert waste from the landfills of the Yukon," effectively making Yukon a "Zero Waste society!" (Raven Recycling, n.d.-a).

A strategic plan to set clear directions for its operation was developed in 1993. After three years of operation, Raven Recycling had a budget of $600,000, cash flow exceeding $1 million and a staff of fifteen. Raven was processing nine commodities in the recycling centre, with the society playing a major role in the implementation of the Yukon government's Beverage Container Regulations. Raven was also involved in numerous activities to reduce the Yukon waste entering landfills (Graham & Associates Management Consultants, 1993). With these increased activities and demands, the requirement for a plan and management approach was evident. It was recognized that the recycling industry was relatively new, with many unknowns, so it would be difficult to determine long-range activities. At that time, Raven was seen to be a useful policy tool by government that would support government goals (Graham & Associates Management Consultants, 1993).

By 2004, Raven's revenues were $2,023,883, with expenditures of $1,908,290, and in 2010 the revenues were up to $2,834,113, with total expenditures of $2,766,660. Over the years, the expenditures for charitable programs are generally over two-thirds of its total expenditures, with the remainder for management and administration costs.

During the next two decades, the recycling committee would grow into the Raven Recycling Society, a large-scale compost and recycling operation that employs more than twenty full-time staff and accepts over thirty different commodities for recycling. It demonstrated early in its development that it was a rapidly growing entity that could adapt readily to change in uncertain times, proving its capacity for future operations.

Current Operations

The following is a list of Raven Recycling's current roles:

1. bottle refund depot (beverage containers);
2. recycling centre for paper, plastics, glass, tin cans, scrap metal (in addition, there is scrap-metal processing and recycling, as well as a "free store" for people to drop off and pick up items);
3. community service provider to educate and increase awareness of issues of waste, recycling and the importance of this area (Raven provides recycling bins for community events and pickup services for paper, cardboard and beverage containers from local businesses);
4. private contractor with a number of operations, including the compost facility and gatehouse at the city of Whitehorse landfill, waste audits and waste expertise and administration of the Yukon government's Recycling Club for Children Program (the latter is provided in collaboration with Environment Yukon [now Community Development] and has been a great way to involve children and youth in recycling).

The Raven Recycling Society is a registered nonprofit society and charitable organization with an established constitution and bylaws. It does not receive core government funding and reinvests any profits back into its operations to support the community. It does this by ensuring that "any surplus funds from recycling profitable commodities (such as aluminum) are spent on recycling items that lose money (such as magazines)" (Raven Recycling, n.d.-a). Surplus is also allocated to research, consulting, public education and advising governments about the dangers of waste and the benefits of recycling. Raven diverts about two thousand tonnes of waste from the Whitehorse landfill site each year. Diversion credits from the city of Whitehorse support operations, providing $50/tonne toward the processing and shipping of eligible recyclable materials, with a cap of $100,000. This only provides part of what is spent annually on shipping, processing and building costs. This is estimated to be about $400/tonne, with plastics being $126/tonne to ship out and paper at $107/tonne. There has been a continued increase in people bringing materials to the centre, and Raven now provides recycling for about thirty different household commodities. Raven Recycling has a Papersave program, with commercial pickup service for paper, corrugated cardboard and various other commodities. In 2008, Raven was awarded $15,000 from the Yukon government's waste reduction and recycling initiative for the purchase of a truck for this program.

If you talk with people working at the centre, they will tell you that the current building for operations is inefficient and its size limits any capacity for growth. Operations today are close to capacity, but there are opportunities for further development. Raven has applied for special project funding through some of the Yukon government programs to build the capacity of this enterprise and meet the ever-growing needs and interests of the community.

In addition to employing twenty-six staff, there is a full-time paid executive director who works with ten volunteers on the board of directors. While most of the staff work at the recycling centre in the industrial area of downtown Whitehorse, two Raven employees work at the city of Whitehorse landfill. An education coordinator works in collaboration with Industry Canada on the Computers for Schools program and the Recycling Club, respectively. These programs, along with regular presentations brought into schools by the education coordinator, help raise awareness of waste processing and other environmental issues among the children and youth of Yukon. Raven does the administrative work on behalf of the Yukon government for the Recycling Club initiative, which includes participants between the ages of four and sixteen from all Yukon communities (Rifkind, 2009b). The Computers for Schools program provides young students who otherwise would not have access to computers with computers that would otherwise end up in landfills. This national, federal-government-led program began in 1993 but was undertaken by Raven in 2010. The program collects, repairs and refurbishes donated surplus computers from government and private-sector sources. Having started out as a simple bottle depot, Raven's operations are now divided into four different roles.

Impact in the Community

In the last twenty-two years, Raven Recycling has had enormous success diverting huge amounts of waste from landfills, educating the public on recycling and environmental issues and providing paid employment opportunities to the community. By using profits made on refundable products (bottles and cans) to pay for recycling items that lose money (magazines), Raven is effectively subsidizing recycling in Yukon, thus saving the municipal government's money. Raven Recycling's contribution to the community is even more impressive when considering the fact that in virtually every other municipality in the country, taxpayers typically pay for these services.

With the aid of public relations campaigns, Raven has been able to provide easy access to information on recycling and its many other services. The recycling centre, in the industrial area of downtown Whitehorse, also serves as a hub for smaller recycling centres in rural Yukon communities. The impact that Raven has had throughout Yukon over the last two decades can be quantified by looking at Whitehorse's landfill diversion data and the annual recycling totals of Raven Recycling itself.

Figure 14.2 illustrates how the amount of recycling and compost diverted from Whitehorse's landfill has increased steadily over the past ten years. In 2000, Raven diverted 229 tonnes of compost and 1,116 tonnes of recyclable material from the landfill. In 2010, 2,149 tonnes of compost and 2,678 tonnes of recyclables were diverted. That is a 938 per cent increase in compost diversion and a

14.2 Waste Diverted through Composting and Recycling in Whitehorse, 2000–2010

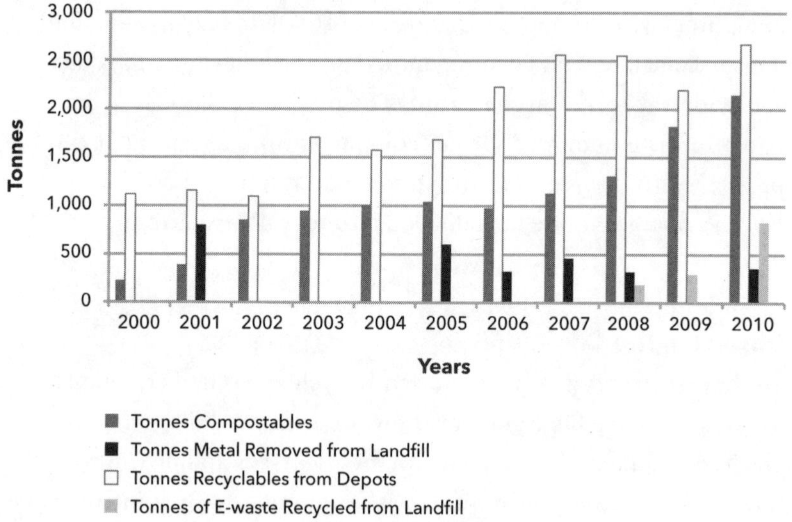

14.3 Recyclables, Refundables and Scrap Metal Collected by Raven Recycling, 2001–2010

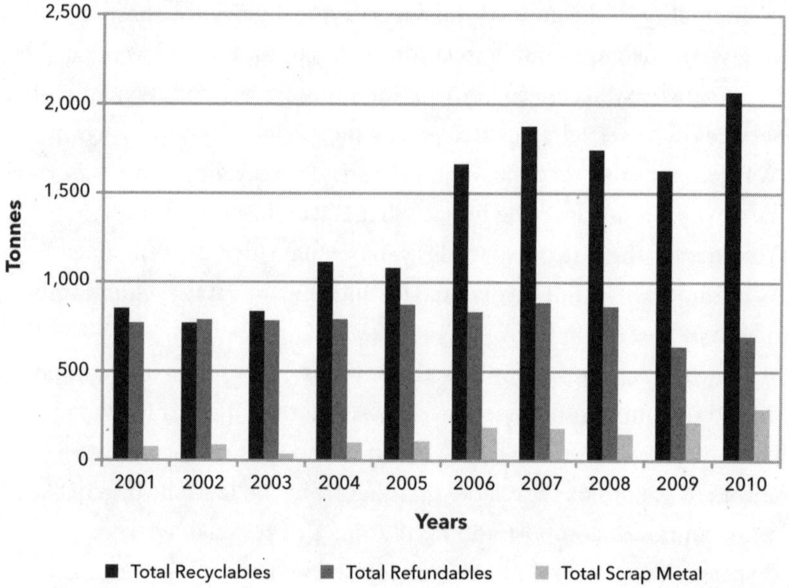

240 per cent increase in recyclable material diversion over a ten-year period. These numbers unambiguously demonstrate that Raven Recycling has been increasingly successful in its pursuit of decreasing the amount of waste that ends up in the landfill. In addition, Raven began recycling computers, printers and other types of electronic waste in 2009 and managed to divert twenty-five tonnes of electronic waste from the landfill in 2010.

Figure 14.3 shows that while the amount of recycling that Raven has processed has increased from 853 tonnes in 2000 to 2,069 tonnes in 2010, the total refundable material processed has, in fact, remained relatively stagnant and actually decreased from 772 in 2000 down to 698 in 2010. This can be explained by the fact that recycling services have been expanded over the years and more products are being accepted. Joy Snyder, the executive director of Raven Recycling, has noticed that "across the country, bottle and can recycling numbers are steadily declining because the ten cent refund simply isn't enough anymore" (personal communication, July 2011). Joy hopes to see the ten-cent refund increased in the near future in order to provide further incentive for people to bring in their bottles and cans.

An interesting quirk of the Yukon recycling trade is that the society is one of the territory's largest bulk exporters. In 2009, Raven shipped the equivalent of 550 semi-trailers worth of loose recyclables outside of Yukon for recycling and reuse (Raven Recycling, n.d.-a).

Challenges and Future Prospects

In Yukon, a social enterprise leads in key aspects of the provision of recycling services. In terms of financial support, this is often an area of struggle for social enterprise operations. Revenues and capital generally come from customers, credits unions and chartered banks, investors, members, employees or owners, government and donors (Vink, 2010). As with other nonprofit recycling organizations, Raven works closely with the public and governments to achieve its intended goals. Support and program development occurs in cooperation with the Whitehorse municipality and Yukon government to ensure that it not only continues operations but is able to expand. In many jurisdictions, governments take the lead role and responsibility to ensure recycling programs are in place. For example, in the Northwest Territories, the Department of Environment and Natural Resources implements programs to recover, reuse and recycle waste products/materials throughout the territory. The department has established a website and funding for specific programs and initiatives provided as part of the implementation of the territory's Waste Reduction and Recovery Act.

Recycling organizations across Canada that use nonprofit, socially oriented business models are proving to be leaders that take a firm stand on reaching substantial waste management objectives such as zero waste. Governments may not always be supportive of recycling initiatives and activities. For example, the Nunavut government recently cancelled a recycling pilot program for beverage containers when it concluded that the costs of recycling outweighed the benefits. Yet in the community of Rankin Inlet, it found that the recycling project cleaned the streets of pop cans and provided residents with a source of income (Windeyer, 2011). There is another social enterprise that has now stepped in to fill this gap and develop recycling programs in Nunavut. Arctic Co-operatives Ltd. announced in June 2011 that it would be launching a Nunavut-wide recycling program for aluminum cans (Windeyer, 2011).

Raven Recycling has faced many challenges over the years, often because of financial limitations. With continued growth and an ever-increasing interest in recycling by the community, it is reaching its capacity with limited abilities for expansion. Without room to grow, it is not able to handle more recyclables. There are limitations in terms of space, staff and machinery. A new building is necessary to expand operations and allow for greater diversion of waste from the landfill. It has almost reached capacity at the current facility that has been in use for more than ten years. The board of directions would like to see a new building that operates quite differently from current operations. It would be known as a material recovery facility. This

14.4 New sorting bins for various types of recyclable materials at Raven Recycling, 2014.
Courtesy of Valoree Walker

type of facility allows for efficient sorting, processing, compacting and storage with specifically designed equipment and machinery. This would save time, money and enhance recycling capacity for Yukon. Part of the enhancements would include the implementation of a blue box collection system.

Raven would like to see Whitehorse become the entity responsible for recycling. The city could undertake this responsibility by providing a service contract with financing to provide consistent support for recycling work in the community. This would provide opportunities for expansion. The financial crisis of 2008 revealed how vulnerable Raven can be to fluctuations in global commodity prices. There was recognition that the volunteer board members of Raven are liable for what has become a multimillion-dollar business (J. Snyder, personal communication, July 2011). Even with the public support and individuals donating their refundable materials to support the sustained operations of the facility during the financial downturn, it has become evident that governments need to play a more substantial role in the recycling sector.

Raven needs to work in partnership with the Yukon government and Whitehorse to create policies that deliver material to the recycling centre. One suggestion has been to have legislation that bans the dumping of cardboard and compost at the landfill. Construction, demolition and commercial waste account for over 90 per cent of the waste in the landfill site (Kerr, 2011). The federal government is working on an extended producer responsibility, meaning that the producer pays for the disposal at the end of the product's life. This initiative started in Europe and is making its way to Canada.

Community involvement in recycling has increased significantly, with people committed to recycling and reducing waste. Raven is lobbying for zero waste. It is a philosophy that encourages project designs and processes that turn common trash into resources (Kerr, 2011). According to the Zero Waste International Alliance, the concept behind zero waste is to conserve and recover all resources and not to burn or bury them (City of Whitehorse, n.d.). The city of Whitehorse and the Yukon government have agreed to a goal of zero waste by 2040 and 50 per cent waste diversion by 2015. The diversion goal meter shown on the city of Whitehorse waste diversion page shows that as of June 2015, it has reached 33 per cent of its goal. Raven would like to see the territory adopt more policies that encourage zero waste. In the solid waste action plan of 1995, there was a goal of 50 per cent diversion by 2000—a goal that was not met. Rather, Yukon has stagnated diversion at 11 per cent for many years (Snyder & McInroy, 2011).

In 2009, the Yukon government undertook an extensive review of its solid waste operations with the objective of modernizing and improving solid waste management in the territory. One of the objectives was to work in partnership with municipalities, communities, industry and stakeholders to develop a coordinated, regional approach. A solid waste advisory committee has been established to explore innovative and long-term improvements to recycling, diversion, reduction and handling, as well as to increase public participation in waste management solutions (Yukon

Department of Community Services, 2011). A new action plan is a first step in improving waste management activities in Yukon. Approximately 75–80 per cent of waste can be recycled or composted (Snyder & McInroy, 2011). In Yukon, there is the desire to recycle more, but the recycling industry cannot afford to support these desires as it requires more infrastructure and a clear strategy for solid waste management (Kerr, 2011).

Raven continues to challenge Yukon to strive toward a zero waste society. As Dr. Paul Connett stated at a recent presentation in Whitehorse, when it comes to recycling, especially industrial and commercial, Whitehorse is way behind (Keevil, 2012). We need to decide if our solutions are going to be designed for corporate interests or the community's interests (Keevil, 2012).

In 2014, Raven Recycling experienced significant changes to its operations. In October, the Raven Recycling board of directors officially announced that it was shutting down Raven's free public drop-off for nonrefundable recyclables. They had lobbied governments since 2008 to develop a solid funding framework to support the recycling of nonrefundable materials. These nonrefundable materials include cardboard, paper, plastics, Styrofoam, milk cartons, Tetra Paks and tin and make up 90 per cent of the current recycling stream. The diversion credits from the city of Whitehorse and Yukon government cover less than half the cost of processing these materials. The costs of recycling refundable materials are covered under the Beverage Container Regulations, but these make up only about 11 per cent of the total volume of materials currently processed (Raven Recycling, n.d.-b). Without any source of stable funding to cover the increasing processing and shipping costs, Raven determined it was no longer feasible to continue this side of its operations.

This change is partially a result of Raven Recycling losing its long-standing service contract with the city of Whitehorse to run the gatehouse operations at the Whitehorse landfill. This provided $170,000 annually to its operations. Even after providing a lower bid, it was still higher than the business that was awarded this contract in

January 2015. This has affected Raven's staffing and impacted other areas, as these funds had been one way that it was able to hire an education coordinator and educate schools and the public.

As a social enterprise, Raven Recycling had made enough money in the past, but the low commodity markets and loss of revenue in some service contracts created challenges for the board to carry out its mandate. Having the ability to respond to the market and alter its operations is one advantage of a social enterprise. Raven continues to serve as a beverage container depot, paper-save program and scrap metal dealer. It has subsidized recycling since 1992, but local and territorial governments need to play a greater role to sustain and expand recycling in Whitehorse. There is also a private recycling business in Whitehorse, but it operates in a different manner from this social enterprise. It does not provide education programs, it does not have a mortgage (because it has not invested in infrastructure) and, up until Raven's closure, it processed a much smaller volume of nonrefundable items.

Raven Recycling had also closed the free public drop-off because it had stockpiled tonnes of paper and plastics that it could not afford to ship out for recycling. As part of a short-term deal, the Yukon government and city of Whitehorse agreed to help both recyclers ship out their stockpiled materials. The Yukon government contributed more than $500,000 in short-term funding in April 2015 to support the recycling processers with an additional $68,000 for shipping stockpiled mixed plastics. The city of Whitehorse also committed an additional $57,300 in diversion credits and advanced the $150,000 set aside for 2016 diversion credits (Yukon Government, 2015). These temporary measures allow for continued operations while long-term solutions and plans are developed. Raven Recycling reopened its public drop-off bins for nonrecyclables, and operations will continue while the municipal and territorial governments consider sustainable ways to manage recyclables.

To be more competitive in current times, Raven Recycling recognizes it needs to be adaptable and responsive. Raven will continue to operate and look for other opportunities and supports that will allow it to continue to fulfill its mandate and improve operations. As the pioneer of recycling and waste reduction in Yukon, Raven Recycling continues to tackle the challenges it faces. As a social enterprise, Raven is committed to making sure the community interest takes precedence over profits and that it will be here for a long time.

Authors' Note

We would like to thank the following staff members of Raven Recycling for providing information for this chapter: Executive Director Joy Snyder and former employee Robin Reid-Fraser.

References

CBC News. (2009, May 28). Raven Recycling gets $320,000 from Yukon government. Retrieved from http://www.cbc.ca/news/canada/north/story/2009/05/28/raven-recycling-funding.html

CBC News. (2015, April 18). Whitehorse's Raven Recycling to reopen after funding increased. Retrieved from http://www.cbc.ca/news/canada/north/whitehorse-s-raven-recycling-to-reopen-after-funding-increased-1.3039145

CharityFocus Imagine Canada. (n.d.). Raven Recycling Society. Retrieved from http://www.charityfocus.ca/EN/Pages/CharitySummary.aspx?CharityID=128565884RR0001

City of Whitehorse. (n.d.). Department of Sustainability, Waste Diversion. Retrieved from http://www.whitehorse.ca/departments/environmental-sustainability/waste-diversion-847

City of Whitehorse. (2010). Engineering & Environmental Services. Retrieved from http://www.city.whitehorse.yk.ca

Demonstrating Value. (2009, April 4). *The Demonstrating Value initiative: Developing the Demonstrating Value framework*. Retrieved from http://www.demonstratingvalue.org/sites/www.demonstratingvalue.org/files/uploads/DV_research_initiative_detailed_report.pdf

Dolphin, M. (2014, December 12). Raven Recycling worries about loss of landfill gatekeeping work. *Yukon News*. Retrieved from http://www.yukon-news.com/news/raven-recycling-worries-about-loss-of-landfill-gatekeeping-work/

Government of Canada. (2009, January 16). Government of Canada supports recycling in the Yukon (press release). Retrieved from http://ainc-inac.gc.ca/ai/mr/nr/j-a2009/nr00000159-eng.asp

Government of Yukon. (2015, March 31). Government of Yukon and city of Whitehorse increase support for recycling (press release). Retrieved from http://www.gov.yk.ca/news/15-111.html#.VVuHYJO_YXg

Graham & Associates Management Consultants. (1993, February). *Raven Recycling Society strategic plan*. (PAM 1993-412). Yukon Archives, Whitehorse, YT.
Hopper, T. (2008, November 21). Raven Recycling calls for bailout from city. *Yukon News*. Retrieved from http://yukon-news.com/news/10315/
Keevil, G. (2012, February 17). Trash-talking Whitehorse waste. *Yukon News*. Retrieved from http://www.yukon-news.com/business/27160
Kerr, J. (2011, April 8). Taking out the trash. *Yukon News*. Retrieved from http://yukon-news.com/business/22564
Munson, J. (2010, October 29). Companies with a conscience in the North. *Yukon News*. Retrieved from http://www.yukon-news.com/business/20237
Raven Recycling. (n.d.-a). About us. Retrieved from http://www.ravenrecycling.org/24-2/about-us
Raven Recycling. (n.d.-b). Closure. Retrieved from http://www.ravenrecycling.org/closure
Raven Recycling. (n.d.-c). Zero waste. Retrieved from http://www.ravenrecycling.org/zero-waste
Rifkind, L. (2009a, June 26). When bad governments do good. *Yukon News*. Retrieved from http://www.yukon-news.com/news/13386
Rifkind, L. (2009b, November 6). Recycling season. *Yukon News*. Retrieved from http://www.yukon-news.com/opinions/columns/15295
Ronson, J. (2015a, April 15). Raven mulls re-opening drop-off recycling bins. *Yukon News*. Retrieved from http://www.yukon-news.com/news/raven-mulls-re-opening-drop-off-recycling-bins/
Ronson, J. (2015b, April 17). Raven Recycling to reopen drop-off recycling bins. *Yukon News*. Retrieved from http://www.yukon-news.com/news/raven-recycling-to-reopen-drop-off-recycling-bins/
Snyder, J., & McInroy, P. (2011, November 25). Getting halfway there. *Yukon News*. Retrieved from http://yukon-news.com/letters/25994
Tremblay, C., Tuberlet, J., & Peredo, A.M. (2010). United we can: Resource recovery, place and social enterprise. *Resources, Conservation and Recycling, 54*, 422–428.
Vink, J. (2010). *From need to opportunity building vibrant rural communities*. Cannington, ON: Social Enterprise Rural Alliance, Brock Community Health Centre.
Windeyer, C. (2011, May 9). Arctic co-ops to launch Nunavut recycling program. *NunatsiaqOnline News*. Retrieved from http://www.nunatsiaqonline.ca/stories/article_print/22133
Yukon Department of Community Services. (2011, Summer). Yukon solid waste action plan update. Retrieved from http://www.community.gov.yk.ca/cd/solidwaste.html

15

Kiri Staples and Valoree Walker

Volunteer Bénévoles Yukon

The Case for Volunteer Centres

There are more than one hundred volunteer support centres operating across Canada, but there is only one that is still operating in the North. This is Volunteer Bénévoles Yukon (VBY), an organization that has been in operation for ten years. It is similar to other volunteer centres, with its primary goal to foster and develop volunteerism in communities, but it continues to diversify and respond to the needs of Yukon groups to maintain its viability as an organization. Volunteer centres are focal points for volunteerism, providing a broad range of supports and services that meet the needs of the communities they serve.

As we have become more aware of the contribution of volunteers to society, there has been greater recognition for the importance and need for support centres. Recent statistics show that 13.3 million people in Canada volunteered nearly 2.1 billion hours in 2010, the equivalent of nearly 1.1 million full-time jobs (Vézina & Crompton, 2012). There is no question that the voluntary sector is a significant contributor to the economy. Volunteers and volunteerism have been described as the heart of social capital (De Raad, 2003). The International Year of Volunteers in 2001 and the Canada Volunteerism Initiative (CVI) created heightened recognition for the social and economic contributions of volunteerism. De Raad (2003) highlights the profound impacts made by volunteers through the example of the Global Polio Eradication initiative that was spearheaded by UNICEF, Rotary International, the US Centers for Disease Control and Prevention and the World Health Organization. In 2011, after twenty-three years of operation, this initiative has involved two hundred countries and twenty million volunteers enabling the immunization of 2.5 billion children. This shows what is possible with volunteer efforts and the significance of their impacts.

Having a facility that serves as a support hub is critical for volunteers and volunteer organizations in order to maximize the potential of their contributions to communities. These centres promote and coordinate volunteer efforts and provide resources for a broad range of organizations. With their knowledge of the sector, they are able to tailor services and provide sector-wide solutions, and through their networks they share information and resources to strengthen and improve organizations. They also play a key role in advocating on behalf of the nonprofit groups they serve for policy changes at various levels of government (Sabin, 2011).

Yukon has a high number and broad range of social economy (SE) organizations contributing to the well-being and sustainable development of communities (Southcott, Walker, Wilman, Spayor, & MacKenzie, 2010). As one of these SE organizations, Volunteer Bénévoles Yukon understands the nature of its operations and limitation factors, particularly those that rely heavily on volunteers. It is able to support a broad range of nonprofit organizations, as well as the public sectors, with targeted programs and outreach. VBY has grown and expanded its services, membership and initiatives, but it is also an organization that is currently wondering about the sustainability of its own operations. Over the years, its role has evolved, yet still today it remains a crucial part of the SE sector and remains optimistic about its future. This is a case that is similar to other SE organizations that continue to operate but with constant uncertainty on funding supports. VBY has experienced both ups and downs but has continued operations despite the challenges it has faced and continues to face. It continues to look at options that allow it to grow as an effective support hub to meet the needs of Yukon communities. This case highlights the integral role of government and partnerships for social economy organizations to function effectively.

History

The first Canadian volunteer centre was established in 1937 in Montreal in response to the Second World War and the need for volunteers (Volunteer Canada, n.d.). Volunteer centres have continued to develop in Canada, offering programs and services to support the volunteer sector in cities, communities and regions. These centres are nonprofit organizations or groups dedicated to fostering and developing volunteerism in communities, and they reach across the nonprofit and public sectors (Ontario Volunteer Centre Network, n.d.). Volunteer centres generally provide a range of programs and services, including:

- promoting volunteerism and raising awareness of the power of the service;
- building local volunteering capacity;
- connecting people with opportunities;
- building capacity through training of volunteers/managers of resources and other nonprofits;
- providing supports and resources to volunteers and volunteer organizations;
- advancing the role of volunteers in providing services and meeting community needs;
- advocating on issues relating to volunteers and volunteer organizations and other nonprofits; and
- administering program funds.

The concept of volunteer centres in the North is relatively new. The Northwest Territories (NWT) developed a nonprofit volunteer centre that operated from December 2003 to June 2008 through funding support from the Canada Volunteerism Initiative. It was not able to continue once funding ended and the territorial government was not able to provide core-funding support. However, the situation has been different in Yukon, with a greater connection between the territorial government and VBY that has allowed for sustainable operations and the development of more activities and programs to support volunteers.

The idea for a Yukon centre began in 1998 with a feasibility study by the United Way Society of Yukon, identifying a need among nonprofit and nongovernmental organizations (NGOs) for a central management office. Four years later, this gap was filled by the creation of the Yukon Volunteer Bureau, which began operations in April 2002. Initially a pilot program of the United Way Society of Yukon, the volunteer bureau was funded by the Yukon territorial government under the Community Development Fund. In 2004, the organization became its own entity as a registered nonprofit society, later registering as a charitable organization. Run by a volunteer board, its membership base was opened broadly to the public, with some restrictions for political parties and/or religious groups. The mission of the Yukon Volunteer Bureau was set out clearly: "to foster and promote volunteerism throughout the Yukon by providing easy access to resources, training, consultation, and support for individuals and organizations" (Volunteer Bénévoles Yukon, n.d.). Its initial vision of a "strong Yukon with a strong volunteer spirit" (Volunteer Bénévoles Yukon, n.d.) was supported by offering services such as a volunteer matching system, training for board members and a resource library.

Over the last six years, VBY has obtained funding from a variety of sources to support administrative requirements and projects of the organization. Funding to support its work has come primarily from government, with nominal funds from membership fees, training fees, donations and other sources (see Figure 15.1). In 2005,

15.1 Funding Sources for Volunteer Bénévoles Yukon, 2004-2012
Source: Volunteer Bénévoles Yukon *Three Year Final Report* (2008-2011)

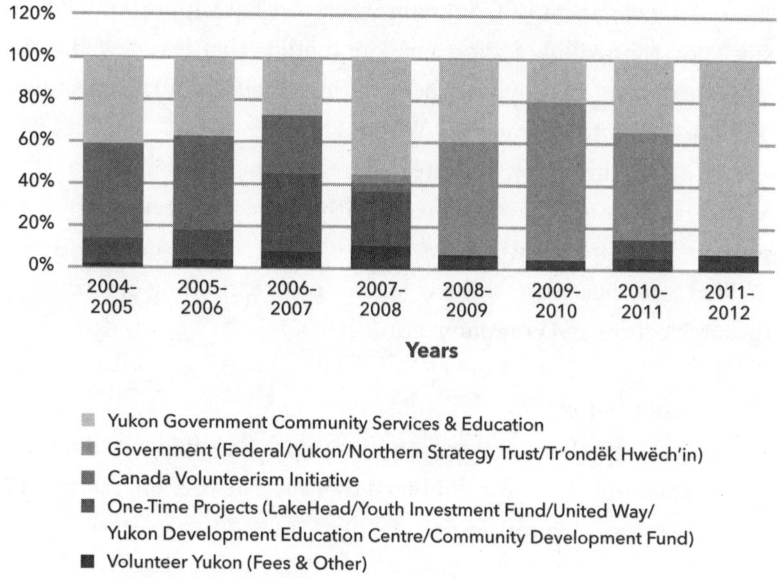

the Yukon government provided $202,500 over three years for its operation. The proposal was to have the Yukon government funding decline as the Yukon Volunteer Bureau matured (Government of Yukon, 2005).

Figure 15.1 shows the percentage of revenues from government, donations, membership and other sources since 2004–2005 (Volunteer Bénévoles Yukon, 2011b). The organization received funds through the Canada Volunteerism Initiative (2004–2007), and then in 2008 it received a contribution from the Northern Strategy Trust Funds to resume full operations. Funds from the Yukon government have increased in the last few years, corresponding to specific projects that VBY administers. This includes the Nongovernment Organization Training Fund (NGOTF) that was established in 2011. This fund, managed by VBY, provides $50,000 annually to nongovernmental organizations on behalf of the Yukon government's Department of Education, the division of Advanced Education. Yukon's Department of Community Services has supported VBY since 2004, providing $67,000 in core funding that is renewed annually, and part of this pays for the part-time position of the executive director (Volunteer Bénévoles Yukon, 2011b).

In 2009, the Yukon Volunteer Bureau changed its name to Volunteer Yukon/Bénévoles Yukon, with enhanced services to support Francophone Yukoners. Its programs and projects are now divided into four centres: the volunteer centre, training centre, resource centre and communication centre.

VOLUNTEER CENTRE

- Provides a volunteer management system (involving a volunteer database of over 250 volunteers) that matches organizations and volunteers to opportunities.

TRAINING CENTRE

- Provides public training for board leadership or customized training via NGOTF.
- Provides risk management training for NGOs being developed through a partnership with Imagine Canada.

RESOURCE CENTRE

- Provides a lending library with books, journals and newspapers on topics supporting development and management for non-profit organizations.
- Provides podcasts—audio broadcasts with training, discussion panels and interviews on topics such as board roles and responsibilities and risk management. These enable Yukon communities access if they are not able to travel to attend sessions.
- Provides checklists that help NGOs and nonprofits to assess their own organizations in areas such as office management and treasurer duties, fundraising practices and reporting to the Canada Revenue Agency.

- Provides a professional services database that holds contact information for trainers and consultants who are interested in working with nonprofit organizations.

COMMUNICATION CENTRE

- Provides NonProfitNet, which is a list-serv that serves as a networking tool for nonprofit organizations as well as the wider volunteer community. NGOs and volunteers advertise events, ask for help and offer tips on fundraising, financial management and more. It allows organizations to make connections across distances and collaborate with others they may not have previously worked with. It now contains over 290 members.
- Provides volunteer recognition, including providing details on the Volunteer Experience Recognition Program (VERP), which is a standardized, Canada-wide certification that can help students, new Yukon residents or mature workers find a job or enter post-secondary education.
- Provides e-newsletters, radio shows and presentations to government and nonprofit organizations.

As Yukon's only volunteer centre, VBY represents the territory and maintains a connection to the national volunteer sector through its membership with Volunteer Canada. Volunteer Canada is the country's primary voice for volunteerism. Through various programs and projects, research and training, it seeks to support and increase participation in the volunteer sector. It also aims to foster a national dialogue on issues related to volunteerism by connecting with volunteer centres, community organizations, national organizations and businesses. As a member of Volunteer Canada, VBY is able to engage in this dialogue, as well as provide input as a representative of the North.

Impact on Community

After ten years of supporting and providing a variety of services to Yukon's volunteer and nonprofit sector, Volunteer Bénévoles Yukon has demonstrated its impact on the NGO community and the people of Yukon. Informally, VBY has become a call centre of sorts, helping NGOs and individuals to connect and answering questions where possible. The importance of this role is evidenced by numbers alone; in 2010–2011, VBY was contacted over five hundred times and supported over 154 NGOs from a variety of sectors (Volunteer Bénévoles Yukon, 2011c). At the 2011 VBY annual general meeting, a three-year (2008–2011) final report was presented that highlighted VBY's accomplishments, providing statistics for training, volunteers, resources and membership. Since VBY began as an independent organization in 2004, it has served over three hundred NGOs, which is more than half of all the nonprofit and volunteer organizations in the territory. The number of memberships has also steadily increased, with VBY claiming 144 members in 2011.

VBY strives to build a stronger volunteer environment through training that builds the skills and knowledge of those working in the voluntary and nonprofit sector. Training and resources were expanded through a three-year funding partnership with the Tr'ondëk Hwëch'in First Nation that began in 2009. This enabled the hiring of a training manager and volunteer manager to support these activities. The VBY's training centre has also made a considerable difference in Yukon's nonprofit sector. For Doug Caldwell, who has been a board member for VBY for three years and is the current vice president of the board, "many more NGOs are more properly trained and organized so they can deal more effectively with their primary mandated roles and the benefits they provide to communities and the people in them" (personal communication, July 2011). In other words, "they are better at what they do." Since 2009, 730 board members, staff members and volunteers have participated in workshops provided by VBY. In 2010–2011, VBY offered twelve workshops that brought together a total of 156 participants. With both public and customized training sessions offered, topics have ranged from strategic planning to writing funding applications to First Nations committee member training. Feedback from these workshops has been extremely positive, with 94 per cent of those attending indicating they found these to be useful (Volunteer Bénévoles Yukon, 2011c). VBY has also been able to provide funding to nonprofit organizations through the NGO training fund. This is important in the context of Yukon, where many of the territory's social economy groups struggle with access to consistent revenue sources. In 2011, there were a total of twenty-eight applications, with fifteen of these approved for funding to support training initiatives for Yukon NGOs.

However, VBY's executive director points out that the impact of the training programs might only be short-term. Whether participants actually use the knowledge they gain from the workshops for a more lasting change is unknown, as these organizations often have high staff and board turnover so knowledge and expertise may not be retained by an organization. Furthermore, the impact that VBY has had has largely been limited to the Whitehorse area, as it is difficult and more costly to provide the same opportunities in less accessible rural communities. Nonetheless, Volunteer Bénévoles Yukon has been working to change this disparity by offering services online that will work for everyone, such as webinars, checklists and podcasts. The high staff turnover in these types of organizations also emphasizes the need for ongoing training supports for new individuals.

There is also supporting evidence of impacts through the numbers of volunteers and how these compare on a national level. Statistical information was not collected for the North before 2004, but numbers from Statistics Canada (Imagine Canada, 2012) surveys since then show that Yukon had one of the highest volunteer rates in 2007 (58 per cent) (see Table 15.1). Although this number has dropped to 49 per cent in the 2010 survey, the Yukon results continue to be above the other territories and close in line with volunteer rates in the provinces. The Yukon volunteer rate in 2010 was higher than the other northern territories, with the Northwest Territories and Nunavut showing the lowest volunteer rates in Canada

(37 and 41 per cent, respectively). In both the Northwest Territories and Nunavut, the territorial governments now have the primary responsibility to support and develop volunteerism, as they do not have volunteer support centres. This may be one factor contributing to lower volunteer rates.

15.1 Canadian Volunteer Rates for the Provinces and Territories from Statistics Canada Surveys Conducted in 2004, 2007 and 2010

	Volunteer Rate (% Population)			Average Volunteer Hours		
Province	2004	2007	2010	2004	2007	2010
Yukon	52	58	49	196	176	131
Northwest Territories	53	46	37	153	151	173
Nunavut	42	43	41	132	186	152
National	45	46	47	168	166	156
British Columbia	45	47	50	199	172	178
Alberta	48	52	55	175	172	140
Saskatchewan	54	59	58	188	147	143
Manitoba	50	54	53	155	159	141
Ontario	50	47	48	162	164	164
Quebec	34	37	37	146	162	128
Newfoundland & Labrador	42	46	52	188	176	155
Nova Scotia	48	55	54	195	183	207
Prince Edward Island	47	56	56	163	147	157
New Brunswick	44	48	49	185	175	154

Challenges

Of course, VBY's operations have not been without their challenges. "Funding, funding, funding" is how the VBY director describes the organization's main obstacle (B. Bourdache, personal communication, July 2011). Caldwell echoes this by stating, "VBY could advance further, but as we live with an annual funding allotment, our continuation into the future is not a given...we would very much like to make it so" (personal communication, July 2011). In 2007, this problem became all the more apparent when VBY lost half of its funding. As a result, between 2007 and 2008 it could not offer some of its usual services. Although the organization was still technically in operation, its sole purpose was to find funding. Fortunately, these efforts were successful and VBY received a three-year funding contract from both the Yukon government's Northern Strategy Trust and the Tr'ondëk Hwëch'in First Nation in 2008.

Like many nonprofit organizations, Volunteer Bénévoles Yukon faces further challenges within the sector. Creating lasting partnerships can be especially difficult, with numerous social economy organizations in Yukon all vying for limited funding opportunities. While VBY is attempting to overcome these attitudes of competition and create more cooperation, it recognizes that it takes time to change the way things are done. A lack of awareness also contributes to the challenges of establishing local connections. Executive Director Bruno Bourdache explains that although the organization has worked hard on communications and outreach, individuals and organizations are not always reaching out when they could be. In the future, Bourdache hopes that these relationships will be recognized and the benefits understood.

The most recent set of challenges for Volunteer Bénévoles Yukon is primarily financial. Once again, the extent to which the organization can operate, and even whether or not it will continue to exist, relies on its precarious funding situation. June 2011 marked the end of the three-year funding provided by the Northern Strategy Trust and the Tr'ondëk Hwëch'in First Nation. Consequently, the organization no longer had the means to retain its training manager or volunteer manager. VBY has had to significantly cut back on the services it provides, reducing its capacity to support other SE organizations. This is part of the wider funding problem in the territory, one that countless social economy organizations are familiar with. Few funders offer core funding, preferring instead to provide resources on a project-by-project basis. As a result, the overstretched staff of these nonprofit groups must spend a significant amount of their limited time and resources finding and applying for a range of different funding sources.

Further problems arise when funders change their funding criteria. Organizations are faced with the challenge of having to follow these guidelines yet maintain their core values and mandates. Some groups, such as Volunteer Bénévoles Yukon, do their best to get away from this funding dependency by generating revenues. In the case of VBY, this independent revenue stream currently makes up only a small portion of its budget, through fees for membership and training workshops. In the future, however, it is looking to increase this source of funding. VBY's executive director maintains that in the short term, Volunteer Bénévoles Yukon can maintain its operations. It continues to seek out funding opportunities and remains hopeful for continued operations in the future. Without additional funding, VBY may be forced to once again stop its services and focus only on fundraising. Worse yet, it may have to close its doors permanently.

Unfortunately, the predicament that VBY finds itself in is not a unique one. Similar trends in the challenges that Volunteer Bénévoles Yukon faces are apparent across the North, often with less fortunate outcomes. A primary example of this is Volunteer NWT. The organization began in December 2003 as part of the federal Canada Volunteerism Initiative and operated under a similar mandate as Volunteer Bénévoles Yukon. It developed information and resources; connected volunteers and voluntary groups; shared training information, ideas and best practices; promoted funding opportunities; explored cross-sector unity strategies and built cross-sector governmental and business community relations (Campbell &

Sladowski, 2009). The Department of Municipal and Community Affairs (MACA) of the government of the Northwest Territories (GNWT) was an active member and provided matching funding in 2004. There was strong government support when this began, with the territorial government developing a Volunteer Support Initiative (VSI) that included a declaration on volunteering and a vision, principles and goals, with a four-year action plan that committed the GNWT to a stronger relationship with volunteers and volunteer organizations (Campbell & Sladowski, 2009). In 2008, however, Volunteer NWT was forced to close its doors after the CVI closure and the final funding of $50,000 from the GNWT ended. Although those behind Volunteer NWT were among the most experienced volunteers in Yellowknife, the board felt that without core funding from the government, there was no way the organization could effectively provide services to the entire territory. Moreover, the board lacked the foundation of basic infrastructure, such as an office, required to apply for corporate funding. Again, part of the problem was that the territorial government did not provide continued and sufficient funding given the sheer number of social economy organizations competing for it.

A few months after Volunteer NWT closed, the GNWT indicated that it would improve the long-term voluntary sector presence in the territory. In March 2009, MACA held a volunteer summit to provide an opportunity for consultation with volunteers and to gather input for improvements to supports for volunteers and voluntary organizations. This was to strengthen the sector with the intention to create a 2009–2012 GNWT Volunteer Support Initiative (Northwest Territories Department of Municipal and Community Affairs, 2009). There were also public consultations on the VSI in 2010. Although the results of the consultation and updated VSI are not available, other information on the MACA website shows continued but limited supports to the sector through its Volunteer Organization Development Contribution, volunteer awards program and Northwest Territories Fire Service Merit Awards. Having volunteer operations run through MACA does have limitations, as the volunteer initiative is just one aspect of MACA's many operations, so support for this sector may not get the necessary attention needed. MACA has focused on volunteer promotion. It has offices in various NWT communities and this provides for a broader network to support volunteers. The national volunteer numbers for 2010 indicate that volunteer numbers are significantly reduced in the NWT. It is difficult to assess the state of volunteerism in the NWT, and without a volunteer centre, there are no collective efforts or advocacy to support and build the sector. As indicated by Sabin (2011), reviving a policy and advocacy network is the best option for promoting government policies that create an amenable operating environment for the voluntary section. Volunteer NWT had created an extensive website resource that was still available online until 2011, but it is now no longer accessible. Aggie Brockman, who was the coordinator of Volunteer NWT, hopes that eventually people will recognize the value of such an organization. In order for this to be realized, however, high levels of support from within the government are necessary.

Developments and Future Prospects

Volunteer Bénévoles Yukon has continued to diversify and respond to the needs and changes in Yukon, which is key for its continued operations. Over the years, the role of VBY has shifted in response to the needs of Yukon volunteers and the nonprofit sector. It now works toward servicing NGOs and their staff, as opposed to strictly supporting volunteers. Following a number of surveys and questionnaires directed at VBY's clients, it was able to focus services on more effectively addressing the concerns of NGOs in the territory.

VBY has become more proactive in its activities. Despite funding problems, it continues to operate on ambitious terms. Along with its daily operations, the organization has been evaluating the potential for a service centre for Yukon's NGOs. This would allow those in the nonprofit sector to pool resources, such as bookkeeping, project management, proposal writing, evaluation, equipment and training (Volunteer Bénévoles Yukon, 2011a). In doing so, these organizations would be able to collaborate more efficiently and effectively and improve performance standards. This would also free up more time and reduce costs so that NGOs could focus more time and energy on their primary mandate and less on administrative tasks. In 2010, VBY received funding from the Yukon government to conduct a feasibility study to examine whether this project would be possible. The results of this study demonstrated that while there is certainly interest in the creation of a service centre, NGOs are not yet ready to participate in such a project.

In order to build the capacity of nonprofit and nongovernmental groups to eventually take part in the proposed service centre, VBY has implemented Project Water Cooler. As the name suggests, this project will bring together social economy groups through regular informal meetings to discuss the daily challenges they face and successes they accomplish in the course of their activities. This not only means that organizations will be better able to communicate with one another but it will also facilitate networking opportunities. This project is in line with the direction that Caldwell hopes to see VBY take in the future by assisting in more volunteer-oriented services and events. He points out that "as the volunteer knowledge base grows and matures, more skilled volunteers will add value to more organizations and their events" (D. Caldwell, personal communication, July 2011). A recent pan-Canadian study found that fostering meaningful volunteer engagement in Canada today is not just a capacity issue but also a strategic one that must evolve with the trends to meet the needs of both organizations and volunteers themselves (Volunteer Canada, 2010). Keeping current with understanding volunteers and organizational requirements is critical for sustaining an effective and vibrant voluntary sector and in providing the necessary supports as those provided by centres like Volunteer Bénévoles Yukon.

Although much of its work is still done by request, attempts at forging partnerships are actively being made, and these are producing promising results. For example, a previous partnership brought Volunteer Bénévoles Yukon together with the Tr'ondëk Hwëch'in First Nation, which provided funding to VBY for three years. Now that the foundation for a relationship with the Tr'ondëk Hwëch'in has been established, VBY hopes to continue this collaboration in the future. VBY has also been in discussions with Yukon College with ideas on developing a service training course. This would cover more than volunteering, requiring students to look at the broader issues that surround volunteerism and volunteer organizations.

Another main factor to the continued operations of VBY has been its partnerships with the Yukon government. Government support is critical to operations, but to be effective, VBY needs to be independent of government, with the ability to provide dedicated services and advocate on behalf of the voluntary sector in an independent manner. Across Canada, greater recognition has been given to strengthening the relationship between governments and the nonprofit/voluntary sector over the past few years (Campbell & Sladowski, 2009). Increased linkages and greater communication have created more collaborative opportunities and ways to leverage collective capacity. Leaders from provincial and territorial governments, as well as the nonprofit/voluntary sector, came together in 2008 and 2009 to examine linkages, exchange information on experiences and determine ways to establish new relationships. An updated snapshot of the voluntary sector for all the provinces and territories provided a summation of the key developments with respect to the process of developing relationships between government and the sector (Campbell & Sladowski, 2009). These provided examples of government-nonprofit relationships and factors that contributed to successes or failures in particular jurisdictions.

In the NWT summary, it was noted that after the closure of the Volunteer NWT centre, there was optimism that the GNWT would take a lead role to improve the long-term voluntary sector presence in the territory. It was soon recognized that without a volunteer support hub there were limitations to the extent of the reach to the voluntary sector by government. In other provincial jurisdictions governments are looking at ways to strengthen relations with the nonprofit sector. One recent example is the Partnership Project initiative in Ontario. This is a dialogue, which began in 2010, that is happening between the Ontario nonprofit sector and the Ontario government. The Ontario government is seeking advice and ideas on ways to renew, streamline and modernize the relationship between government and Ontario's nonprofit sector, focusing on improved collaborations, potential policy and legislative frameworks, funding mechanisms, new finance approaches and more effective methods of co-ordinating policy, research, communication and practice (Ontario Ministry of Citizenship and Immigration & the Ontario Trillium Foundation, 2011). There is recognition for the substantial volunteer contribution made in Ontario, with 2004 statistics showing that more than five million people donated 819 million hours of their time through volunteering and that this is a value equivalent to 400,000 full-time jobs. A recent, in-depth, environmental scan of the volunteer centre service providers in Ontario offers recommendations for ways to move forward, looking from the strengths and opportunities that exist (Luchuk, 2008). Recommendations and tools were developed and compiled to support volunteer centre services in the province. Such initiatives show the interest for government partnerships and supports for the sector.

Many factors contribute to successful operations, but being responsive to needs and the ability to diversify operations are critical factors for sustainability. Volunteer centres generally provide a range of programs and services in response to community needs and, as such, many have had a long history. New initiatives and recent research shows that these centres may also serve as a link between volunteering and employability (Rochester, 2009), adding to the list of potential services they might provide. The fact that Volunteer Bénévoles Yukon continues to work toward expanding the support it offers to the nonprofit sector, in spite of the looming threat of funding cuts and closure, is a testament to the dedication and will of those behind the organization. Moreover, this persistence is all the more important given the experiences of similar organizations across the Canadian North, such as Volunteer NWT. VBY has survived through such challenges before, adapting its role and its services when need be, and has proven to be a truly resilient organization.

Authors' Note

We would like to thank the following people for providing information for this chapter: Bruno Bourdache, the executive director of VBY; Doug Caldwell, the vice president of the VBY board; and Aggie Brockman, former coordinator of Volunteer NWT.

References

Campbell, M., & Sladowski, P. (2009). *Building sustainable relationships between non-profit/voluntary sector and provincial & territorial governments: An updated pan-Canadian snapshot and summary report of the second gathering of counterparts.* Ottawa, ON: Centre for Voluntary Sector Research and Development, Carlton University.

De Raad, A. (2003). Volunteerism, the heart of social capital. Retrieved from http://www.unv.org/en/about-us/who-we-are/leadership/executive-coordinator/executive-coordinators-news/doc/volunteerism-the-heart-of.html

Government of the Northwest Territories. (2005). *Declaration on volunteering.* Retrieved from http://www.maca.gov.nt.ca/sport/volunteerism/VolunteerDeclarationPoster.pdf

Government of Yukon. (2005, April 15). Volunteers grow community, April 17–23 is volunteer week (press release #05-103). Retrieved from http://www.gov.yk.ca/news/05-103.html

Imagine Canada (2012, March). *Research note: Caring Canadians, involved Canadians: 2010.* Retrieved from http://sectorsource.ca/sites/default/files/research_note_csgvp_tables_03212012.pdf

Luchuk, L.C. (2008). *Building stronger organizations: In-depth environmental scan of volunteer centre service providers in Ontario.* Retrieved from http://sectorsource.ca/resource/file/building-stronger-organizations-depth-environmental-scan-volunteer-centre-service

Northwest Territories Department of Municipal and Community Affairs. (2009). *Volunteer summit report.* Retrieved from http://www.maca.gov.nt.ca/resources/2009_Volunteer_Summit_Report.pdf

Ontario Ministry of Citizenship and Immigration & the Ontario Trillium Foundation. (2011). *The partnership project: An Ontario government strategy to create a stronger partnership with the not-for-profit sector 2011.* Retrieved from http://www.citizenship.gov.on.ca/english/pp/about.shtml

Ontario Volunteer Centre Network. (n.d.). About the Ontario volunteer centre network (OVCN). Retrieved from http://www.ovcn.ca/about.aspx

Rochester, C. (2009). *A gateway to work: The role of volunteer centres in supporting the link between volunteering and employability.* London, UK: Institute for Volunteering Research. Retrieved from http://www.volunteercalgary.ab.ca/pdfs/gateway_work.pdf

Sabin, J. (2011). *Yellowknife's voluntary and nonprofit sector: A portrait of a northern social economy* (Social Economy Research Network of Northern Canada, Research Report Series RR#2-2011). Retrieved from http://ycdl4.yukoncollege.yk.ca/sernnoca/resources/research reports

Southcott, C., Walker, V., Wilman, J., Spavor, C., & MacKenzie, K. (2010). *The social economy and Nunavut: Barriers and opportunities* (Social Economy Research Network of Northern Canada, Research Report Series RR#1-2010). Retrieved from http://dl1.yukoncollege.yk.ca/sernnoca/resources/researchreports

Vézina, M., & Crompton, S. (2012). *Volunteering in Canada* (Statistics Canada Catalogue no. 11-008-X, Canadian Social Trends). Retrieved from http://www.statcan.gc.ca/pub/11-008-x/11-008-x2012001-eng.pdf

Volunteer Bénévoles Yukon. (n.d.). About Volunteer Yukon. Retrieved from http://www.volunteeryukon.ca/spip.php?rubrique15

Volunteer Bénévoles Yukon. (2011a). *Annual report: Review of 2010/2011 operations*. Retrieved from http://www.volunteeryukon.ca/IMG/pdf/AGM_2010-2011_Annual_Report.pdf

Volunteer Bénévoles Yukon. (2011b). *Three year final report 2008–2011*. Retrieved from http://www.volunteeryukon.ca/IMG/pdf/Volunteer_Yukon_3-yr_Final_Report.pdf

Volunteer Bénévoles Yukon. (2011c). Results-based report July 2010–April 2011. Retrieved from http://www.volunteeryukon.ca/IMG/pdf/2010-2011_Statistics_Report.pdf

Volunteer Canada. (n.d.). Volunteer centres. Retrieved from http://volunteer.ca/i-want-volunteer/volunteer-centres

Volunteer Canada. (2010). *Bridging the gap: Enriching the volunteer experience to build a better future for our communities*. Retrieved from http://volunteer.ca/study

16

Frances Abele and
Chris Southcott

Conclusion

Fifteen years ago, Kathy Brock (2001) identified a "fundamental change in the relationship between government and society...in western liberal democracies....[T]he role of non-governmental organizations is becoming more central to the very practice of democratic governance" (p. 263).[1] The case studies in this book vividly illustrate this change, revealing multiple connections between each organization and northern democratic development. They also reveal much about what is important to northern community residents.

Cultural vitality is important. For nine of the fourteen social economy organization profiles in this book, contributing to cultural vitality is an explicit goal, and for the remaining five organizations it is at least a welcome consequence. For example, Beaudoin's study of the Labrador archive and magazine *Them Days* highlights the importance of individual initiative and collective community effort in the face of the changing priorities of public funders and increasingly precarious funding. Consistent effort by a handful of committed individuals in the forty years of *Them Days*' existence created a rich resource of cultural materials now maintained by a new generation. Similarly, Christensen's short history and appreciation of Folk on the Rocks describes a vital community institution that has developed and grown in Yellowknife since 1980, the project of a small team of imaginative individuals who have attracted many volunteers and local business support. The Folk on the Rocks music festival has grown, attracting artists from all over the North, southern Canada and other countries, while it has expanded to provide an important resource for local musicians between festivals and an important venue for northern arts and crafts.

Northerners have also turned to social economy organizations to further local economic diversification. The Torngat Fish Producers' Co-operative was formed by local fishers after the government of Newfoundland and Labrador decided to sell its fish plants to foreign investors. The co-operative purchased the facilities and has for over thirty years managed the purchase and marketing of a shifting array of marine food products. Boutet's review of the history of Torngat illustrates the ways in which the co-operative has responded to changing market conditions while maintaining its capacity to provide seasonal local employment and a means for fishers to sell their products. The people of Repulse Bay also relied upon the co-operative form, founding the Naujat Co-operative in 1968, part of the wave of community co-operative establishments across the North. While Naujat, in common with most other northern co-ops, experienced financial difficulties, particularly in the 1970s and 1980s, today it is an important and stable economic institution in Repulse Bay. Alsop notes that it is the third-largest employer in town, engaged in retail sales, purchasing of handicrafts and art, construction, tourist accommodation and the provision of community cable services.

Two cultural institutions focus on sales of artistic production. Since 2002, the Yukon Artists @ Work Co-operative has provided a Whitehorse retail sales venue for a varying number of Yukon artists, with membership rising as high as forty-four artists in some periods. Staples's biography of the co-operative is a story of commitment and struggle—of survival and development in the face of volunteer shortages, vacillating local business support and an inclement territorial policy environment. For the life of Yukon Artists @ Work, there has been no territorial government support for co-operatives. The importance of financial support is evident in the history of Nunavik Creations, an artisanal clothing manufacturing company supported by Makivik Corporation and the Kativik regional government. The company provides training in sewing, an important traditional skill, and obtains materials for sewers, thus supporting harvesters. In addition, the company supports the fabrication and marketing of original designs, thus building upon traditional skills to develop a niche in current markets. While financial stability is maintained by the beneficiary organizations' readiness to support Nunavik Creations, Drouin and Moisan's study details the challenges the company faces, on the one hand to train and retain sewers, and on the other to develop a sufficient market for its products. Nunavut Creations is an example of a business created to meet certain social objectives—local employment, skills preservation and development, cultural continuity—while it finds a way to flourish in the market economy.

In addition to enhancing cultural vitality and economic diversification, the social economy organizations in this book also play important roles in social service and in providing public policy advice and advocacy.

The Labrador Friendship Centre responded to the social needs created by the 1960s and 1970s resettlement of Inuit and Innu from their small settlements and from the land to the comparatively larger centre of Happy Valley-Goose Bay. An initiative of community activists from the Labrador Inuit Association and the Company of Young Canadians, the Friendship Centre provided a range of services to the new residents, as it continues to do. An even older organization, formed with similar purposes, the YWCA in Yellowknife has provided housing, education, advocacy and all manner of support to women in Yellowknife since 1966.

Smaller northern communities have created service-providing organizations uniquely adapted to their needs, reflecting community priorities and preferred approaches. The three organizations of this type profiled in this book all build upon the traditional strengths of Inuit communities—social solidarity and mutual care. The Unaaq Men's Association of Inukjuak, described by Villaseñor-Caron, provides a structure for Elders to mentor and educate younger men in the community. Unaaq takes advantage of funding opportunities as they become available to launch initiatives that strengthen the social fabric of the community and support the intergenerational transmission of values, providing Inuit-style training and education in a wide range of traditional skills. Johnson's portrait of the Ilisaqsivik Society of Clyde River presents an Inuit-led, community-based organization working to bridge economic development and healing and cultural activities. The society aims to meet a range of community needs through a family resource centre, Ittaq Cultural Heritage and Research Centre and Tukumaaq, Inc., a profit-taking entity intended to meet the need for visitor accommodation while generating a revenue stream to support the other activities. One of the largest employers in Clyde River, at the time of writing, Ilisaqsivik provided work and training to twenty full-time employees, eighty-seven part-time and sixty-seven casual workers. Illiniariuqsarvik Head Start in Igloolik, the third community-based social service organization profiled in this collection, is also an important community employer, with more than thirty staff members. Kennedy Dalseg describes the role of Illiniariuqsarvik as an important social hub. Originally created out of community concerns over low levels of attendance among elementary school children, today it offers a variety of programs for preschool-aged children, as well as supports for parents and other caregivers. Unaaq, Ilisaqsivik and Illiniariuqsarvik are remarkable examples of community-led and developed organizations, resilient and adaptable, and all playing a role in meeting social needs while sustaining ties among community members. All take advantage of some external funding (and respond to funding opportunities with alacrity), but they depend for their long-term survival upon the commitment of staff and volunteers.

An organization that straddles service provision and public advocacy, with a strong element of business development, is Raven Recycling, based in Yukon. Walker, Moise and Staples describe the organization's inventive and opportunistic approach to sustainable waste management and the encouragement of environmentally responsible behaviour. The Inuvik Community Greenhouse, profiled by Christensen, represents another community organization of this type—providing in its community greenhouse and composting programs a practical means for community members to act on their knowledge of sustainable subsistence activity while taking a leadership role in public education.

Alternatives North is an enduring Yellowknife-based coalition of volunteer social activists who have a research-based approach to contributing to policy discussions in the Northwest Territories, best captured in its catch phrase, "persistent and consistent." Active since the early 1990s, the organization is formally incorporated but operates with no paid staff and consensus-based decision making. Sabin's conclusion is that Alternatives North will continue to intervene on matters such as the politics of income inequality, social justice and sustainable economic development.

Closing Observations

Social economy organizations in northern Canada play a vital role in sustaining cultural vitality, contributing to community economic diversification, providing culturally appropriate social services and contributing to public discourse through research and advocacy. The following Table 16.1 provides an overview of their distribution across these realms of activity.[2]

16.1 Major Goals of Social Economy Organizations and Institutional Form

Major Goals/ Institutional Form	Co-operative	Nonprofit Society	Not-for-Profit, Nongovernmental Aboriginal Organization	Company
Cultural Vitality	Yukon Artists @ Work	Folk on the Rocks; Them Days	Labrador Friendship Centre; Ilisaqsivik Society of Clyde River; Unaaq Men's Association of Inukjuak; Illiniariuqsarvik Igloolik Head Start	Nunavik Creations
Economic Diversification	Naujat Co-operative; Yukon Artists @ Work; Torngat Fish Producers Co-operative	Raven Recycling	Ilisaqsivik Society of Clyde River; Tukumaaq, Inc.	Nunavik Creations
Social Service	Naujat Co-operative	Inuvik Community Greenhouse; YWCA Yellowknife; Raven Recycling	Labrador Friendship Centre; Ilisaqsivik Society of Clyde River; Unaaq Men's Association of Inukjuak; Illiniariuqsarvik Igloolik Head Start	Nunavik Creations
Social Advocacy, Policy Research and Advice	Torngat Fish Producers Co-operative	Alternatives North; Inuvik Community Greenhouse; YWCA Yellowknife; Raven Recycling		

We believe that the examples of social economy organizations in this collection are intrinsically interesting. Certainly, their organic relationship to, and their value in, the communities that have founded them is as obvious as it is various—from heritage preservation and development, to social service and social reform, to public advocacy. Such organizations deserve more attention for the essential role they play in evolving democratic institutions and practices in northern Canada. The formal institutions of northern liberal democracy include public bureaucracies, legislatures and judiciaries but also many northern innovations, including Aboriginal governments, beneficiary organizations, co-management boards and other institutions of public governance. Northern liberal democracy also depends upon dozens of social economy organizations, a selection of which are profiled in this volume.

The northern social economy institutions in this collection display the range of activities and the diversity of approaches taken by community members to solve local problems, relying upon local assets and various institutional forms as appropriate to their situations. For almost all of the organizations profiled in this volume, securing adequate and stable funding is a major preoccupation. As is the case all over Canada, social economy organizations in the North are kept afloat through a combination of volunteered work; support in cash and in kind from Aboriginal organizations, unions, companies and governments; grants; and own-source revenue generation. The challenges inherent in this situation are at once exacerbated and ameliorated by a northern location: exacerbated because of the high cost of rent, fuel, transportation, communication and salary (if any can be paid) in northern, particularly Arctic, locales; ameliorated because of the strong traditions of self-reliance and community volunteerism characteristic of northern communities.

In all their diversity, the social economy organizations identified in this volume share these circumstances. For most, a more conscious and supportive territorial or provincial policy program framework would be a boon, capable of delivering stable and predictable core funding along with a public recognition of the essential role played by these citizen-centred organizations.

Notes

1. A complementary argument was made a few years later in Laforest and Phillips (2007).
2. The categories of activity discussed here are a simplification of the typology developed in our earlier work, published in Southcott and Walker (2009). A comparison of the 2009 portrait of the social economy with the cases highlighted in this volume suggests that our sample is representative of the range.

References

Birchall, J., & Ketilson, L.H. (2009). *Resilience of the cooperative business model in times of crisis* (International Labour Organization Report). Retrieved from http://www.ilo.org/wcmsp5/groups/public/---ed_emp/---emp_ent/documents/publication/wcms_108416.pdf

Brock, K.L. (2001, July 1). Democracy is coming: The new interest in NGOs, civil society and the third sector. *The Philanthropist, 16*(4), 263–271.

Laforest, R., & Phillips, S. (2007). Citizen engagement: Rewiring the policy process. In M. Orsini & M. Smith (Eds.), *Critical policy studies* (pp. 67–90). Vancouver, BC: UBC Press.

Southcott, C., & Walker, V. (2009, Spring). A portrait of the social economy in northern Canada. *The Northern Review, 30*, 13–36.

Wuttunnee, W., Chicilo, M., Rothney, R., & Gray, L. (2008). *Financing social enterprise: An enterprise perspective.* Retrieved from http://community-wealth.org/content/financing-social-enterprise-enterprise-perspective-working-paper

Wuttunnee, W., Rothney, R., & Gray, L. (2008). *Financing social enterprise: A scan of financing providers in the Manitoba, Saskatchewan and Northwestern Ontario region.* Retrieved from http://ius.uwinnipeg.ca/WIRA/wira_final-reports.htm

Contributors

Frances Abele is a professor in the School of Public Policy and Administration at Carleton University, and the academic director of the Carleton Centre for Community Innovation. She was coordinator for SERNNoCa Theme 3: The State and the Social Economy in the North.

Jennifer Alsop has completed her master's degree in public administration at the School of Public Policy and Administration at Carleton University. Her research, "The Role of the Cooperative Enterprise in the Social Economy of Repulse Bay," looked at the changing role of the co-operative sector in Repulse Bay as community members adapt to new and evolving environmental, governance and economic realities.

Matthew Beaudoin conducted research with the Labrador Métis during the completion of his master's degree at Memorial University in 2008. He received a Ph.D. in anthropology from Western University in 2013 and currently works as a project manager at Timmins Martelle Heritage Consultants Inc. in London, Ontario.

Jean-Sébastien Boutet holds a master's degree in historical, cultural and environmental geography from Memorial University. His current research interests include the historical and contemporary effects of large-scale mineral development for the Aboriginal communities of Quebec-Labrador.

Julia Christensen is an assistant professor of geography at Roskilde University in Denmark and a research fellow at the Institute for Circumpolar Health in Yellowknife, Northwest Territories. Her research focuses on northern Indigenous experiences of home and homelessness across the Canadian North and Greenland.

Cédric Drouin is currently working for Quebec's National Assembly. He holds a bachelor's degree in political science from Laval University and a master's degree in public administration from the École nationale d'administration publique. While studying, he was a research assistant for the Centre interuniversitaire d'études et de recherches autochtones and the Chaire La Capitale en leadership dans le secteur public. Economic development at a local and international level has always been among his academic interests.

Moses Hernandez was born and raised in Yellowknife, Northwest Territories. He attended St. Francis Xavier University, where he completed a bachelor's degree (honours) in political science, and he has completed graduate studies in polar law at the University of Akureyri in Iceland. He is a former Jane Glassco Northern Fellow and is currently studying architecture at Dalhousie University.

Noor Johnson's research examines knowledge politics and environmental governance, with a particular focus on Inuit involvement in climate change research and policy in the Canadian Arctic. As a member of the Energy working group of the Fulbright Arctic Initiative, she has studied knowledge and participatory processes for offshore decision making. Noor holds a Ph.D. from McGill University in cultural anthropology, a master's degree from American University in public anthropology and a bachelor's degree from Brown University in development studies.

Sheena Kennedy Dalseg is a Ph.D. candidate in the School of Public Policy and Administration (SPPA) at Carleton University and a research associate at the Carleton Centre for Community Innovation. The research completed for her chapter was undertaken in 2009 as part of her master's program at the SPPA, which focused on the social economy and community development in Nunavut. In addition to her academic pursuits, Sheena is also co-founding director and editor of Northern Public Affairs, a not-for-profit organization that publishes an online and print magazine of the same name.

Frédéric Moisan is a professional chartered accountant. He studied business administration and accounting at Laval University and Sherbrooke University. He worked in Kuujjuaq in Nunavik, Quebec, between 2006 and 2015 for different social organizations.

Joseph Moise grew up in Whitehorse, Yukon, and studied at Humber College and Carleton University. He studied international relations at the University of British Columbia and worked as a summer student for the SERNNoCa office in Whitehorse.

Rajiv Rawat has been a resident of Yellowknife, Northwest Territories, since 2008, when he began work at the Institute of Circumpolar Health Research and NWT Protected Area Strategy. He currently works at the Prince of Wales Northern Heritage Centre and was elected to the board of trustees for the Yellowknife Education District No. 1 in 2015. Rajiv is also a graduate of Cornell and York universities, where he studied biology and environmental studies, respectively.

Jerald Sabin is a Ph.D. candidate in the Department of Political Science at the University of Toronto. He is a research associate with the Carleton Centre for Community Innovation at Carleton University and the founding editor of *Northern Public Affairs*.

Chris Southcott is a professor of sociology at Lakehead University and the principal investigator and chair of the Resources and Sustainable Development in the Arctic Project. He was the principal investigator of the SERNNoCa Project and coordinator for Theme 1: Profile of the Social Economy in Northern Canada.

Kiri Staples was born and raised in Whitehorse, Yukon. After completing a bachelor of arts in international development studies at Trent University, she completed a master's degree in environment and sustainability at the University of Saskatchewan in 2014.

Lucille Villaseñor-Caron's early work focused on a multidisciplinary approach to social, political, economic and environmental issues affecting all levels of society, from the local to the global level, including several Inuit organizations. As the founder of Happiness & Wellness Therapy, she now works with individuals, groups, couples and families who are seeking support to overcome structural, mental, emotional, physical and/or spiritual challenges. She is also a registered mental health counsellor for Health Canada's Indian Residential Schools Resolution Health Support (IRSR) and Non-Insured Health Benefits for First Nations and Inuit (NIHB) programs.

Valoree Walker has a Ph.D. from the University of Alberta. She is a long-term northern resident, living in Cambridge Bay, Yellowknife, and Inuvik, where she was previously director of the Aurora Research Institute. She was the national coordinator for the SERNNoCa project and is currently the coordinator for the Resources and Sustainable Development in the Arctic project at Yukon College, Whitehorse.

Index

Other Titles from The University of Alberta Press

Crow Never Dies
Life on the Great Hunt

LARRY FROLICK
PAUL CARLUCCI, FOREWORD

304 pages | 25 B&W photographs, 1 map, foreword, index
Wayfarer Series
978–1–77212–085–1 | $29.95 paper
978–1–77212–144–5 | $23.99 EPUB
978–1–77212–145–2 | $23.99 Kindle
978–1–77212–146–9 | $23.99 PDF
Travel Literature | The North | Indigenous Culture

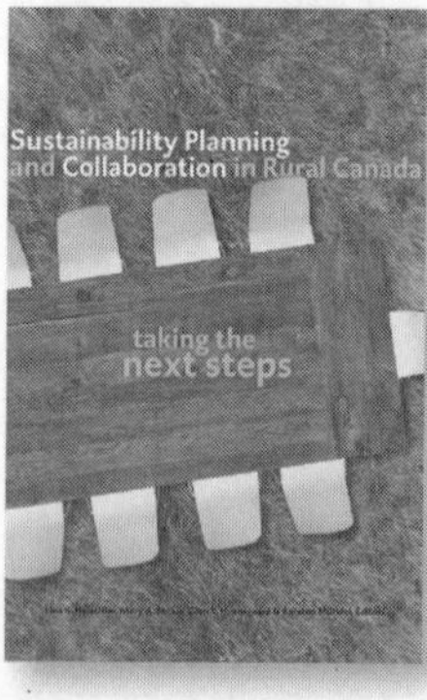

Sustainability Planning and Collaboration in Rural Canada
Taking the Next Steps

LARS K. HALLSTRÖM, MARY A. BECKIE,
GLEN T. HVENEGAARD & KARSTEN MÜNDEL, EDITORS

408 pages | 3 B&W photographs, 5 maps, 5 diagrams, 10 tables, bibliography, notes, index
978–1–77212–040–0 | $49.95 paper
978–1–77212–095–0 | $39.99 EPUB
978–1–77212–096–7 | $39.99 Kindle
978–1–77212–097–4 | $39.99 PDF
Community Development | Rural Canada | Sociology

Idioms of Sámi Health and Healing

BARBARA HELEN MILLER, EDITOR

248 pages | 4 B&W photographs, 1 map, bibliography, notes, index
Polynya Press
Patterns of Northern Traditional Healing Series
978–1–77212–088–2 | $34.95 paper
978–1–77212–104–9 | $27.99 PDF
978–1–77212–105–6 | $27.99 EPUB
978–1–77212–106–3 | $27.99 Kindle
Northern Studies | Traditional Healing | Health